THE   END

OF

PRIVACY

THE END

OF

PRIVACY

How Total Surveillance Is Becoming A Reality

REG WHITAKER

THE NEW PRESS   NEW YORK

Library of Congress Cataloging-in-Publication Data

Whitaker, Reginald, 1943–
    The end of privacy : how total surveillance is
becoming a reality / Reg Whitaker.
        p.   cm.
    Includes bibliographical references and index.
    ISBN 1-56584-378-9
    1. Intelligence service.   2. Privacy, Right of.
3. Information society.   4. Information society —
Political aspects.   I. Title.
JF1525.I6W49   1999
303.48'34 — dc21   98-27826
                                                          CIP

Published in the United States by The New Press, New York
Distributed by W.W. Norton & Company, Inc., New York

Established in 1990 as a major alternative to the large, commercial publishing houses, The New Press is
the first full-scale nonprofit American book publisher outside of the university presses. The Press is operated editorially in the public interest, rather than for private gain; it is committed to publishing in innovative ways works of educational, cultural, and community value that, despite their intellectual merits,
might not normally be commercially viable. The New Press's editorial offices are located at the City University of New York.

www.thenewpress.com

Printed in the United States of America

9   8   7   6   5   4   3   2

Contents

THE END

OF

PRIVACY

Introduction

In the late twentieth century we are told that we live in a new "information economy," that "information is power," and that the key to national success in global competition is to possess the "information edge." We are inundated with both celebrations and warnings about an "information revolution" that is sweeping the world. It is practically impossible for anyone tuned into contemporary media not be aware of the "new information technologies" that are said to be restructuring our political, economic, social, and cultural landscape.

As with much of the end-of-millennium speculation about life in the twenty-first century, there is a great deal of exaggeration and alarm about the new technologies and their implications. Those who issue hard and fast pronouncements about the precise shape of the future are to be disbelieved. However, new technologies and the new media of communication associated with them are having a profound impact, with serious consequences about which we can as yet make only make more or less informed guesses.

As a political scientist, I am particularly interested in the question of power, how it is exercised and by whom. This book focuses particularly on the impact of the new information technologies on political power. I have been especially attracted to a body of theory that looks at *surveillance* as a mechanism of power. Marx incisively analyzed the relationship between economic and political power in the age of capitalism, but left the specific mechanisms, or technologies, of power largely unaddressed. Another line of thought, exemplified in the work of the late French philosopher Michel Foucault, has emphasised surveillance and the strategic use of information as tools of social control. The metaphor of the "Panopticon," which I examine in Chapter 2, is particularly apposite. In our age the lines between the state and society, or between the public and the private sectors, are becoming increasingly blurred, and the state is said to be in retreat. The concept of panopticism has the particular advantage of not privileging formal state power over the informal exercise of power outside the state structures. The latter is a central theme of this book.

I begin in Chapter 1 with a discussion of the role of information in the growth of the twentieth-century state. Intelligence, the purposeful acquisition of secret information, has been an important tool of state power both in war and in peace. Out of this has come a central metaphor of power in this century: the Orwellian state in which totalitarian control is based on a monopoly of information. Even liberal democracies have attempted to imitate some of the features of this model of power. However, the Orwellian model is a radically misleading guide to the structure of power in the next century. The new information technologies challenge us to reconstruct our fundamental notions of power. The state has been decentered, and power is increasingly dispersed and diffused. This does not mean that it weighs less heavily on people, but its origins are now less identifiable, and its effects are experienced very differently.

Chapter 3 looks at the nature of the new information technologies and at some of their implications for society. There is good reason to believe that these technologies have the potential to change drastically our sense of ourselves, and thus to affect in a profound way the concepts of community and citizenship. These changes can be best described as the rise of the network society. To track these changes, I pay particular attention to popular culture, which has, I believe, been especially sensitive to these changes and suggestive about their human impact.

The technical scope of surveillance today and in the immediate future has far surpassed the capacities of the totalitarian states of the immediate past. Chapter 4 presents a survey of some of the new technologies of surveillance being developed and deployed for myriad forms of social control in numerous everyday contexts. These technologies are startling in the degree to which they are now able to render transparent the lives of ordinary people.

The following chapter pursues some of the disturbing implications of data bases, and the power which the possession of detailed data on citizens confers on corporations and states — sometimes referred to as dataveillance. The information society features a new form of alienation: our data profiles are largely out of our control, but they can overshadow and oppress our real selves. Corporate and government institutions are run on the principle of risk management. Data profiles identify people as good or bad risks. Those sorted into the risk category may be excluded from full participation in the economy and society.

Chapter 6 addresses a thorny issue: why is there relatively little public protest against the invasion of personal privacy by the new surveillance technologies and the power of dataveillance? I find the answer to this in the fact that the new form of panoptic power is understood as offering rewards rather than punishments. It is also remarkably adaptable, allowing it to absorb cultural, gender, and other differences. This very adaptability, on the other hand, can encourage fragmentation of the public into multiple "consumer" identities, instead of a common democratic citizenship.

The final chapter looks to the future, and asks what kind of politics is likely to result from the global extension of the new information technologies and rise of the networked society. One plausible model is that of a "virtual feudalism." I reject this model as failing to account for the many negative effects of the new global order, and neglecting the capacity for democratic forces to utilize the new technologies and form global networks of resistance. I also suggest that the instability inherent in the new global order will compel the limited return of states as regulators and enforcers of agreements.

This discussion brings the book full circle. It begins with a discussion of the role of intelligence, and concludes with national security and intelligence agencies cooperating with one another in the policing of the new global order. One of the major effects of the new surveillance has been to diminish the relevance of the Orwellian model of centralized state power. The introduction of the new information technologies has resulted in Big Brother being laid off. Ironically, the instability inherent in the new order may result in Big Brother's services being required once again. This time, however, it will only be as an outside consultant. Power in the networked world will be dispersed and diffuse, but power will continue to play an important part in how that world organizes and sustains itself. How that power is exercised will, of course, be a leading determinant of how humane or inhumane that world is likely to prove. In this regard, much will depend on the will and determination of democratic groups arising out of the new global civil society to form politically effective networks to monitor, criticize, contest, and check the engines of corporate and state power.

I do not offer any blueprints for political opposition. This would be presumptuous on my part, and also premature. What I have tried to do in these pages is to sketch an outline of the changing parameters of power under the impact of sustained technological change, and to suggest some of the consequences and implications.

One further note about what this book does not do. The title refers to the "End of Privacy." New technologies of surveillance are rendering individuals more and more transparent, and relentlessly reducing the private spaces into which people have traditionally been able to retreat for refuge and self-definition. There is good reason to be concerned about this. There are scholars, lawyers, and activists who have developed a body of thinking about privacy protection through regulation and legal safeguards. I do not examine alternative approaches to privacy protection. Different legal systems and different political cultures in Western states render any such discussion a complex exercise in comparative politics and jurisprudence, for which there is no space here. More to the point, the diffusion of new information and surveillance technologies is rapidly transforming the nature of the challenges to privacy protection. In this book, I am more interested in describing the nature of these challenges than in devising specific public policy responses. I do try to indicate the extent of the challenges, which are formidable, indeed.

I would like to acknowledge the invaluable assistance of a Research Fellowship awarded by the Izaak Walton Killam Trust and a research grant from the Social Sciences and Humanities Research Council of Canada, as well as the continued support of my own institution, York University.

1—The Century of Intelligence

T he twentieth century has been the century of Intelligence. It has been many other things as well, a century of astonishing scientific and technological developments and of equally astonishing brutalities and atrocities. But among all the things that distinguish our century from those that have gone before, let us focus for a moment on a particularly intriguing one. Not *i*ntelligence, to be sure, but *I*ntelligence: the systematic and purposeful acquisition, sorting, retrieval, analysis, interpretation, and protection of information. There is no need to put too fine a gloss on this: we are talking about *spying*.

Of course spying is as old as recorded history. According to the Old Testament, "The Lord spoke to Moses, saying 'Send men that they may spy out the land of Canaan, which I will give to the children of Israel. . . .'[1] Lacking God's imprimatur, a former counsel for the CIA has described espionage as the "world's second oldest profession and just as honourable as the first."[2] There have always been secrets, and people have always attempted to uncover them. Spying—with its repulsive yet alluring masks, deception, betrayal of loyalties, and knowledge illicitly gained—has always had its attractions as well as its detractors. And its advantages, too, for stolen secrets have often yielded power and profits for their new owners.

However, it is only in this century that spying has become a systematically organized bureaucratic activity with its own specialized institutional structure, its own technologies, its own scientific knowledge base, and its own semi-autonomous role in global politics. Consider the second world war, the largest global conflict in history, which Sir Winston Churchill described as the "wizard war." Churchill's wizards were mathematicians and academic dons, among them the man who invented the concept of the computer. The wizards were gathered at a secret location in rural England called Bletchley Park where they cracked the codes used by the German military so that Churchill in his command bunker under London's streets could read what the Nazi military were going to do and when they would do it. Other "wizards" in Washington cracked the

Japanese codes, with the result that, in the words of military historian John Keegan, at Midway ("the most important naval battle of the [war]") "knowledge of Japanese intentions allowed the Americans to position their inferior fleet of carriers in such a way as to destroy the much larger enemy force."[3] Intelligence did not win the war for the Allies, but it was a considerable help, just as inferior Intelligence accelerated the decline of the Axis.

With the Manhattan Project and the epochal explosion of the atomic bombs on Hiroshima and Nagasaki in 1945, the significance of Intelligence was racheted up dramatically. In 1945, America held the only key to the secret power of nuclear fission. The Soviet Union dedicated scientific and material resources to their catch-up project, but it also dedicated espionage resources on a large scale. In 1951, at the height of the early Cold War, with Americans fighting Communist soldiers in Korea and Senator Joe McCarthy hunting Communists in America, Judge Irving Kaufman sentenced Julius and Ethel Rosenberg to die in the electric chair for "putting into the hands of the Russians the A-bomb." Their espionage, the judge told the defendants, "has already caused, in my opinion, the Communist aggression in Korea, with the resultant casualties exceeding 50,000 and who knows but what millions more innocent people may pay the price of your treason. Indeed, by your betrayal, you undoubtedly have altered the course of history to the disadvantage of our country."[4] Despite world-wide protests, the Rosenbergs were both duly put to death, leaving two young orphaned sons. The intelligence stakes had become very high.

STATES AND THE LOVE OF KNOWLEDGE

It is impossible to separate the contemporary status of Intelligence from two key features of the twentieth century: dramatic advances in scientific knowledge and its practical application, especially in increasingly lethal military technology; and an international system built on sovereign nation-states, the most powerful of which developed into militarized superpowers. Nation-states, jealously guarding their prerogatives (or pretensions) as sovereign autonomous actors, sought to protect their national security through military strength, either alone or through alliances. Science and the weaponry that could be derived from science were the keys to strength, and hence security. Thus the acquisition of knowledge became a key state activity, in more than one way. Scientists, supported by research infrastructure provided by the state, learned the secrets of nature and applied that knowledge to the secretive development of technology. States also devoted resources to acquiring the knowledge gathered by other states, by voluntary exchange where possible (through alliances) but by aggressive and intrusive collection (espionage) where necessary.

Many have pointed to the perversion of free scientific inquiry: the fruits of scientific research transformed by the alchemy of war and Cold War into national secrets stored within closely guarded arsenals of death. Nowhere was this more apparent than in the development of nuclear weapons. Dr. Robert Oppenheimer, who had been in overall charge of the scientific aspects of the Manhattan Project, grappled with the ethical dilemmas of the uses of the power he had helped unleash, and later questioned the development of the hydrogen bomb. In 1954, his own security clearance was revoked. Yet Oppenheimer's qualms were far more muted than many other scientists. Some atomic scientists, such as Klaus Fuchs, Alan Nunn May, and Bruno Pontecorvo, had even taken matters into their own hands and passed information to the Soviet Union, both before and after the wartime alliance, thus raising ethical dilemmas of a different order. Dr. Albert Einstein, whose earlier theoretical innovations in physics had helped to lay the groundwork for nuclear development, vainly pleaded for peace and cooperation among nations.

Science had been mobilized for war. Intended to restore security in the war of all against all, Intelligence escalated insecurity. Itself increasingly technologized, Intelligence offered the potential to probe ever more invasively into the most closely guarded secrets of the other side, while seductively but deceitfully promising to protect our own secrets. Once settled on this course, states embarked on a vicious circle in which they reached for greater security but grasped only greater insecurity. In a century that saw a veritable explosion of new communications technologies, each technical enhancement of communication called forth new technologies to intercept and read what was being communicated. Following the telegraph and telephone came wiretapping; wireless radio communication prompted the development of new techniques to scoop signals out of the "ether." Communications dedicated for authorized recipients only were encoded to baffle prying eyes and ears, and decryption science was born. Missile technology led to space technology which in turn permitted the stationing in orbit of spy satellites designed to read missile capabilities of hostile states and pinpoint their launching sites for preemptive strikes. The same technology also made it possible to launch weapons of mass destruction from space. Eventually, "Star Wars" technology promised security from attack by a computer-generated anti-missile virtual defence "dome" in the stratosphere. Fortunately for everyone, the collapse of the Soviet Bloc and the end of the Cold War slowed this mad escalator.

The close connection between science, technology, military power, and Intelligence has often been summarized in the maxim that "knowledge is power." There is a lot wrong with this maxim: ignorant power in this century has been known to crush powerless knowledge; and the producers of knowledge have often seen the fruits of their intellectual labor come back to oppress them. Yet for all its ironies and complexities, the maxim has a unique resonance in this century.

This maxim might be amended to fit more precisely the nuances of a technological age. If Intelligence as an organized state or corporate activity is different from intelligence as a quality of mind, so too "knowledge" differs from "information." Knowledge in the older philosophical or religious sense has little or nothing to do with information. The use of scientific knowledge for power through technological development is not at all about knowledge in the older sense. Intelligence has been about the purposeful acquisition of information, that is, specific pieces or bits of "useful" knowledge, rather than knowledge itself. Knowledge becomes information, which in turn becomes "data." Data in computer science is information represented in a form (preferably quantitative) suitable for processing. More generally, data is information organized for scientific analysis or used to make decisions. There can be little doubt that control of this kind of information can yield real power.

THE ODD COUPLE: SPY AND SCHOLAR

There are curious parallels between the worlds of Intelligence and academia. In some cases, the two worlds have come together explosively, as when the brilliant mathematician Alan Turing helped break the German codes at Bletchley.[5] In the United States, academics from the Ivy League universities were important players in the wartime Office of Strategic Services and in the early days of its peacetime successor, the CIA.[6] It has often been said that some of the best minds in the old Soviet Union ended up in the KGB or its various predecessor agencies. There is more to this than some envious attraction of armchair scholars to the shadow world of cloaks and daggers. Intelligence and academia are both in a sense the same business: the systematic and organized collection, analysis, and interpretation of information — and the construction of theories to explain the facts thus processed. Throughout this century, both Intelligence and academia have become specialized and compartmentalized, and external rewards for academic research have increasingly fostered the quantifiable over the qualitative, and data/information analysis over the older notion of knowledge/wisdom. Both Intelligence analysts and academics tend to labor within frameworks that structure and sometimes limit their capacity to understand changing or disconsonant reality. Both are often subject to the frustration of having the powerful, but less knowledgeable, dismiss or ignore their counsels and act in defiance of their advice. The world of Intelligence is studded with horror stories of "Intelligence failures" attributed to willful, ignorant, stubborn political leaders unwilling to listen to what they did not wish to hear, just as the world of public-policy making is littered with academic ideas discarded by politicians in favor of mediocre compromises with wealth and power. Finally, both spies and professors have sometimes been in the uncomfortable, even dangerous, position of telling truth to power.

Three key distinctions remain, however, between spy and academic. First, the information Intelligence is after has deliberately been kept secret. This implies covert collection, which usually mean that spies systematically break the laws of the countries they target. Academics generally pursue open sources of information. Espionage thus regularly touches on a dark side of human nature— lying, deception, betrayal—that may be pathologies of academic life, but are not its routine. Second, Intelligence is a product ordered, produced, and consumed by a single customer, usually the state, and more recently corporations. Academics attempt to publish their findings as widely as possible. If they fail to reach past a tiny initiated audience, the problem is more one of arcane subject matter and exclusionary language than of external constraints. The third distinction is that Intelligence is predicated on hostility among nations, and a competition between them that is not only endemic but potentially deadly. Academic life may be competitive but its ideal, at least, is a peaceful, cooperative pursuit of knowledge.

Beyond these obvious differences, the underlying affinity is extraordinary. The two worlds, with their shared interest in the acquisition and accumulation of information/data as keys to control—of nature and of people and states—have forged a relationship that many find uncomfortably close. The relationship has been particularly fruitful in the technologization of Intelligence toward increasingly sophisticated capacities for sensing, listening, and watching from great distances and across exquisitely constructed defensive barriers—from underwater sonar to listening posts scanning the ether to photo reconnaissance satellites orbiting in space. These advances—like the computer and the Internet—are the product of science and Intelligence working together under military auspices. In fact, the Information Revolution that is sweeping the world at the end of this century owes its genesis, to a large degree, to this odd couple of spy and scholar.

THE WILDERNESS OF MIRRORS

In the Hobbesian world of Intelligence, information is shadowed by its doppelgänger, disinformation; Intelligence by counterintelligence; espionage by counterespionage. As Michael Howard has written, with regard to military Intelligence:

> All surprise rests upon concealment, and "security" is one of the classical "principles of war." But few intelligent commanders have ever been satisfied simply with *concealing* their intentions or their strength. The commander who wishes to impose his will on the enemy—which is, after all, the object of military operations—will seek to *deceive* him; to implant in the adversary's mind an erroneous image which will lead the adversary to act in such a way as to make his own task easier. . . . He will, in short, try to get inside the mind of the enemy commander, assess that commander's appreciation of the position on both sides, and then produce for the enemy, through all available channels, the information that will lead him to make the dispositions which will best conform to his own plan. It is not enough to persuade the enemy to *think* something: it is necessary to persuade him to *do* something. The object of deception . . . is to affect the actions of the adversary.[7]

There have been spectacular examples of deception in the Intelligence game. During World War II, the British were not only able to read German communications, but they were able, through the now-famous "double-cross" system,[8] to "turn" virtually every German spy into a double agent, sometimes complete with a fictitious network, transmitting to the gullible German spymasters only information that British Intelligence wanted the Nazi command to consume. Thus Hitler was given radically misleading indicators about Allied plans and intentions, with dramatic results. For instance, a completely non-existent U.S. Army group pinned down an entire Wehrmacht army in the Pas de Calais in 1944.

During the long years of the Cold War, that quasi-conflict that Mary Kaldor insightfully called the "Imaginary War,"[9] the gossamer skein of lies, counter-lies, and counter-counter-lies that lay between the great Intelligence agencies of East and West, had grown so intricate that some clever minds, charged with trying to unravel the patterns, seem in the end to have gone quite mad. How else to explain the gaunt, haunted figure of James Jesus Angleton, the head of counterintelligence at the CIA, whose hunt for Soviet double-agents grew so frenetic, so undisciplined, and so all-encompassing that the CIA finally sacked him, on the perfectly reasonable assumption that a Soviet mole could hardly do as much damage to the agency and national security as Angleton's own manic mole hunt.[10] Or Angleton's British counterpart, Peter Wright, also sacked for spreading clouds of suspicion, who proudly titled his memoirs "Spycatcher."[11]

Was a defector from the other side what he appeared to be, or was he a plant to spread disinformation? Once set in motion, wheels of suspicion powered an infernal machine. Another striking metaphor has often been used for this strange business: "a wilderness of mirrors". The complexity of reflexive suspicion can be glimpsed in the nuances of the term "*dis*information." *Dis*information is not *mis*information; it is information expertly laced with strategically chosen misinformation. Genuine information is the bait to lure the prey to swallow the hook. But the hook must be carefully hidden and the bait enticing, for the target is, after all, inherently suspicious and discerning. It is not as if every participant does not understand the unwritten rules. Indeed, the other side has its own bait and its own hooks. There is even the dark possibility that, if the other side swallows the proffered bait and seems to be hooked, appearances may be horribly deceiving. Perhaps, as one reels in the prey, it is actually oneself that is being captured through a deception one fatal step more complex than one's own.

In the 1950s at the very heart of the Cold War in divided Berlin, the West built a tunnel under Communist East Berlin to tap into Soviet military communications. The tunnel operated for nearly a year, during which period nearly half a million Soviet conversations were tapped, until the Soviets publicly declared they had discovered the tunnel and the operation came to an end. However, a Soviet agent well-placed within British Intelligence, George Blake, had in fact tipped off the KGB to the plans for the tunnel even before construction began. Still, they let it go ahead and operate for a year. For one thing, the KGB did not wish to alert the West to the existence of the traitor within their ranks. During the time the tunnel operated, the Soviets might have been feeding disinformation to the West to create deceptions and diversions, yet there had to be enough nuggets of good information amid any dross to convince Western Intelligence that the operation was working. According to Western analysts looking back on the period, the yield was rich. As it turns out, the KGB did not alert its parallel military Intelligence agency, the GRU (the real target of the operation in the first instance) of the existence of the tunnel, whether out of inter-agency rivalry or because of a misplaced use of the "need-to-know" rule. Even now, when at least some of the files of the CIA and the KGB have been opened to scholars, and when participants on both sides at the time are ready to more or less freely reminisce about their doings, an irreducible ambiguity remains about who, if anyone, really won in this murky affair.[12]

Once launched into this mirror world, there is no escape from claustrophobia. Or from the very human sense of betrayal necessarily involved in the duplicitous world of human Intelligence. The story of espionage is studded with the names of the great traitors: Kim Philby, Guy Burgess, Donald Maclean, John Cairncross, George Blake, Aldrich Ames: men who lived double lives, appearing to serve their countries but instead clandestinely serving their countries' enemies, who sold out their friends and colleagues, and in some cases may even have delivered agents and sources whose lives were in their trust into imprisonment, torture, and death. A very bad business, no doubt, but one that has generated a literature of fascination, of which John Le Carré's oeuvre is the leading example.

Part of the fascination, aside from that of the dark side of human nature, derives from the very mirror imaging I have been describing. Our traitors are the other side's heroes. And vice versa. There was always a certain ambiguity in how Intelligence defectors from the other side were welcomed in the West. On the one hand, they represented victories over the enemy, especially if they remained in place as double-agents wreaking havoc within rival services. Moreover, by courageously choosing freedom over totalitarianism, they illustrated the moral superiority of our way of life. Yet there remained always a slight residuum of suspicion toward those who had, after all, betrayed *their* country. Moreover, at least at a time when Western moles for the U.S.S.R. still had ideological motives, they too claimed a higher loyalty than country. In the latter years of the Cold War, greed and other ignoble motives began to replace principled devotion to an ideal, however perverted that ideal might seem to those of a different persuasion. It was one thing to be betrayed by Kim Philby, who saw himself as a soldier in a lifelong cause of proletarian revolution; it is quite another to be betrayed by Aldrich Ames, who was paid $1.8 million by his Russian handlers and promised a lavish country *dacha* on retirement. But the exploitation of human weakness—and indeed the use of blackmail as a weapon, especially when based on that old standby, sex—was always near the roots of the spy business, lending some of the same beguiling aura of sleaze and corruption to spy fiction as has always drawn readers to the detective novel. Spying is, to repeat, the "second oldest profession," and thus an ideal frame for tales that linger with fascination over sex, deceit, and death, while drawing suitable moral lessons.

THE AUTOMATION OF INTELLIGENCE

The severe human costs of the spying business, costs shared all around and by all sides, may well have helped confirm a trend through the latter half of the century away from human Intelligence toward automated Intelligence gathering. Signals interception and communications intelligence, technologies still evolving at a exponential pace, have added dazzling extensions to the human ear. Most audio communications can be intercepted by a series of ground-based listening posts linked in a global network. During the Cold War, Western communications intelligence was directed against the Soviet bloc. When the Korean commercial airliner KAL-007 was shot down over Soviet airspace in 1983, the American government immediately was able to provide the media with a complete audio transcript of the conversations between the Soviet pilot who launched the fatal shots and his ground control.[13] This kind of communications intelligence was routine; only its public release was unusual.

Aerial reconnaissance in the early Cold War provided invaluable pictures of military installations inside the Soviet Union, but it was also vulnerable to countermeasures, such as the embarrassing downing of the American U-2 spy plane and the capture of its pilot, Francis Gary Powers, in 1960.[14] The coming of the space age in the late 1950s opened up more secure vehicles for eyes in the sky. At first, spy satellites orbiting the earth produced images that had to be ejected and retrieved, but current models transmit digitized images in real time. High-resolution pictures can distinguish objects on the ground as small as one foot or even less. Apart from their relative invulnerability to counter measures, one of the great advantages of spy satellites is their capacity to obtain different kinds of images by utilizing different portions of the electromagnetic spectrum. Infrared and thermal infrared photography, for instance, can detect and identify features not visible to the naked eye. Thermal infrared can, for instance, point to the presence of buried installations by detecting heat differences on the earth's surface, and both infrared and thermal infrared can "see" at night. Radar imaging can penetrate cloud cover. Computerized image enhancement can analyze imagery and draw out pertinent data while subtracting irrelevant features.[15] Disadvantages of satellite reconnaissance include the high risk involved in launching satellites with expensive payloads (even today, launch failures continue), and the inflexibility and limited targeting that come with fixed orbits. The end of the Cold War caught U.S. Intelligence with an overinvestment in spy satellites fixed on the Soviet bloc. For the turn of the century, a new generation of small intelligence satellites will provide almost constant overhead images of specific trouble spots anywhere in the world.[16] In the post–Cold War era, there have been strong pressures to make the powerful capacities of satellite imagery available to scientific and environmental research,[17] as well as for commercial exploitation, a matter that will be explored in a later chapter.

Technical Intelligence gathering extends further yet. Sensitive seismic monitors record every slight twitch of the earth's crust— and carefully note the exact magnitude of underground nuclear weapons tests. The precise courses of submarines are tracked through the silent depths of the world's seas. All this complex hardware is served by the ever-accelerating capacity for data storage, retrieval and processing, and the development of extraordinarily recondite software to separate "signals" from "noise": for instance, keyword and even voice-recognition "flags" that can pluck the tiny number of nuggets from the limitless volume of dross scooped up by the electronic eavesdropping posts vacuuming communications out of the sky. Or so-called Artificial Intelligence software that can spot money-laundering movements out of the total number of financial transactions occurring at any time on a global scale, by distinguishing anomalous from normal patterns of financial flows.

Automated Intelligence is more expensive than human Intelligence because it is capital intensive, but it has been gaining in popularity, slowly but surely, over its older, traditional rival. Apart from the expansive technological promise, there are certain advantages to replacing human spies with machines. Machines do not knowingly or deliberately lie and deceive and cheat. Nor do they get drunk and blurt out secrets, or land themselves in compromising situations, such as beds with people to whom they are not married. When secrets are passed not through betrayal by trusted associates, but by distant machines scanning the skies and seas and earth, there is also less risk of political complications. Indeed, it gradually dawned on both the United States and the U.S.S.R. that the extraterrestrial Panopticon of spy satellites tirelessly snapping x-rays of the other side's nuclear-strike capacities was actually a stabilizing factor in the superpower confrontation. With both sides professing peaceful, defensive intentions, automated espionage simply confirmed this state of affairs, or at least made it less likely that either side could mount a deadly first strike in secret. Yet if the same Intelligence had been passed by highly placed human moles, there might have been public scandal, with who knows what catastrophic consequences. So the Rosenbergs went to their deaths for allegedly assisting the other superpower to acquire the nuclear capacity to strike the balance of terror that may well have prevented a third world war, while spy satellites circling the earth were credited with building the trust that eventually allowed both superpowers to agree to arms-limitation treaties.

There have been ongoing debates within the Intelligence world about the comparative merits of HUMINT (human-source Intelligence) and TECHINT (Intelligence gathered by technical means). There are clear limitations to the present technology. TECHINT, while excellent for gathering material evidence on such matters as troop deployments and command communications, can probably never get inside the heads of decision-makers and grasp their motives and intentions. It is a matter of some considerable notoriety that the American Intelligence community, despite having its most extensive and sophisticated complex of intrusive surveillance technology focused on the Communist world, failed to foresee the collapse of Communism, the disintegration of the Soviet bloc, and the dissolution of the Soviet Union itself. However intelligent future Intelligence machines may become, human beings program and direct them, and at the end of the day human beings make use of the Intelligence product, or do not, as the case may be. The day of machines entirely displacing human operators remains strictly in the field of science fiction. However, there is no doubt that Intelligence as an organized activity has greatly intensified the development of communications and information technology—and has been itself transformed significantly as a result. In that sense the question of human vs. technical Intelligence is a false alternative: man and machine have been growing together.

GLOBAL POLITICAL POLICING

The Intelligence establishment has gained notoriety, in some cases infamy, for activities other than the gathering of information by covert means. The Americans, with their global reach, turned their hands to a kind of undercover global policing. Interventions in various Third World countries took the form of everything from covertly organized destabilizations to assassinations and coups. Specialized Intelligence skills and resources, ranging from propaganda/disinformation to political manipulation to covert forms of military assistance to rebels, were mobilized to effect actual changes in other countries, instead of just gathering Intelligence. The textbook case was Guatemala in 1954, when the CIA orchestrated a kind of coup by deception, a staged media event that frightened the president into flight and ushered in decades of repressive military rule. Other covert actions were not always as successful (if success in this case is the proper term) but the CIA did gain a global reputation for having its hidden fingers in every pie in every corner of the world, a reputation quite likely out of proportion to that agency's actual capacity for effective mischief.

Superpowers are easily tempted to undertake covert interventions to advance their foreign-policy interests. Networks of agents, sources, and dupes have been carefully constructed, fed, and maintained for intelligence gathering. It is a short step to convert these resources for active use in interventions intended to change the course of events in other countries. Intelligence professionals in the collection and analysis side are not always pleased with what the operations people do, but governments tend to prefer concrete results to yet more analysis. The very special attraction of Intelligence intervention, as opposed to more open forms, has always been that it could be effected secretly. If the intervention succeeded, its sponsors achieved their goals. If it failed, the sponsoring state could avoid the obloquy of humiliating failure. Or so the theory went. In practice, as the CIA and the U.S. government learned to their chagrin, failures did have a way of spilling out into public notice. Nevertheless, controversies and criticisms, and even the end of the Cold War, appear not to have removed the temptation to use covert operations in the service of foreign policy, though media and congressional recriminations in the 1970s have resulted in a formal ban on assassinations of foreign leaders as a tool of American policy.

The increasingly sophisticated technology of Intelligence has also come importantly into play in America's role as global cop. Post-Cold War control of proliferation of weapons of mass destruction depends on the capacity of the U.S. Intelligence establishment's early warning system—its land-sea-air-space surveillance grid—to alert the "world community" to activities by so-called rogue states to develop nuclear, chemical, and biological weapons; to monitor compliance with international arms-limitation agreements by states that already possess such weapons; and to track the movements and communications of non-state actors viewed as actual or potential threats. To be sure, closer human inspection and intervention may be required for enforcement—as witness the wars of nerve between the United States/United Nations and Saddam Hussein's Iraq—but the global technological gaze into every nook and cranny of the earth is the foundation upon which it is predicated.

DOMESTIC POLITICAL POLICING

Undercover political policing on a global scale is only one use (or misuse) to which Intelligence is put. Far more significant for millions of people has been the utilization of the tools of Intelligence for internal security: repression of dissent and dissenters; control of turbulent or "dangerous" classes; compulsory political conformity; and the pervasive and intrusive surveillance and regulation of everyday life. The totalitarian police state stands at one pole; what exists in practice at the other is not a pure "free" society, but a liberal democratic state that contains some authoritarian and illiberal elements. National security, or national *in*security to be more precise, is an anxiety that afflicts states across the ideological spectrum. Intelligence in the service of domestic political policing has been used by governments of all persuasions, and every type of state has relied at least from time to time on secret or political police against the perceived threat of subversion, if not revolution. The incidence and severity of repression has varied a great deal, of course — it would be foolish to equate the witch-hunts of McCarthy-era America, however unpleasant, with the grisly depredations of the Stalinist regimes of the same period, just as it would be inappropriate to match the sporadic transgressions of J. Edgar Hoover's FBI with the routine snooping of the East German Stasi. Yet however different the texture of domestic Intelligence in different regimes, it is the universality of the phenomenon in the twentieth century that is most arresting. The tools for internal surveillance and control being available, no state has resisted the temptation to use them, and few have not attempted to refine the tools yet further. States with many external and internal enemies, real and potential, have often used these tools recklessly and brutally; states with higher degrees of domestic consensus have most often used the tools with greater restraint, discretion, and skill, usually during periodic bouts of national or state insecurity. Such relative restraint, however, has served to mask the negative effects of secret political policing on the practice of liberal democracy.

Fears for internal security and of enemies within tend to be sparked in the first instance by international insecurity. The pathologies of counterintelligence, described above, are intimately linked to the perception of the enemy within as an insidious extension of the enemy without. The "fifth columnist," the spy, the saboteur, the foreign-directed terrorist or subversive: these are images that draw their menace, and fascination, from the blurring of Inside and Outside, of Us and Them. The Cold War image of "reds under the bed" captures this anxiety indelibly. Xenophobia, ideology, and sexual/cultural panic all reinforced one another.

In the years prior to World War I, with the clouds of great power conflict gathering on the horizon, a spy panic swept Britain, fed by the popular press and a new breed of writers who were in effect inventing the modern spy novel. The villains of these novels were German agents intent on undermining British power and security; the heroes were British patriots alert to the secret menace of the Hun within. The British public was aroused to the threat of the internal enemy, defined at this time in clearly ethnic terms, and lurid reports of Hunnish knavery began to circulate.[18] The British state, moved more by such fanciful reports than by concrete evidence, concluded that "an extensive system of German espionage exists in this country, and . . . we have no organisation for keeping in touch with that espionage and for accurately determining its extent or objectives."[19] Accordingly, Whitehall seized the opportunity to create the Secret Service, out of which evolved the external and internal Intelligence agencies, MI6 and MI5. The line between Intelligence reality and Intelligence fantasy was from the start rather blurred, as in a sense it has always remained. Needless to say, similar spy phobias also arose in Germany at this time, with roles reversed, but with similar results.

With the war over and the Hun vanquished, at least for the moment, the new Intelligence agencies turned their attention to a different kind of enemy within, one defined more by ideology than ethnicity. The 1917 Bolshevik revolution in Russia spawned a spectre that was to obsess Western Intelligence for most of this century:

the Communist operative whose domestic revolutionary agenda (bad enough of course in itself) was tied directly to the international threat of the Soviet Union, thus doubling the stakes. For their part, the Bolsheviks pioneered the ruthless use of the secret police as a primary weapon for the consolidation and maintenance of state power, at appalling human cost in purges, arrests, tortures, gulags, and mass murder. The Cheka (Commission to Combat Counter-revolution and Sabotage), eventually to become the KGB, founded what has been called a "counterintelligence state"[20] that made no distinctions between internal security and external Intelligence operations. Bolshevism had no monopoly over police-state forms, as was evident in the Nazi takeover in Germany in 1933, with its Gestapo arm. After Nazism's *Götterdämmerung* in 1945, the eastern half of Germany from the late 1940s to the end of the 1980s combined both Gestapo and Cheka traditions in the Stasi with a surveillance apparatus that penetrated every nook and cranny of civil society, turning friends into informers against friends, even spouses against spouses.[21] The brutality quotient of the Gestapo may have been higher, but for minute detailed efficiency, the Stasi were superior: the ratio of Gestapo agents to citizens was about one to 10,000; by the late 1980s, the Stasi had reached the remarkable ratio of one to 200. Yet both systems failed to sustain themselves.

However repulsive the face of totalitarian repression, we should not turn a blind eye to certain similar practices in Western liberal democracies — themselves national insecurity states — even if qualitatively these features never added up to anything approaching the nightmare of the Nazi or Communist police states. The beliefs common to internal security regimes may be summarized as follows:

An external enemy or adversary is employing a fifth column of agents whose real loyalties, whether for ideological or ethnic reasons, are to the adversary state. The weapons of this fifth column may include espionage, terrorism, sabotage, covert foreign-directed activities of various kinds intended to advance the interests of the enemy, and subversion (the clandestine undermining from within of the integrity and will of the nation and its values). To combat this threat, the enemy within must be identified, isolated, and barred from influence — ideally extirpated altogether, but at the very least watched very closely and contained. To accomplish these goals, it is necessary to develop and maintain extensive surveillance of suspicious groups and individuals, and to build up extensive dossiers on questionable political activity and activists (such dossiers must be cumulative and permit cross-checking or matching with other data bases on citizens and groups). The most effective means of amassing such dossiers is through internal Intelligence networks of agents and sources on much the same lines as external Intelligence networks are formed; both human and technical methods of surveillance are employed as required. Further, what is to be identified is risk, not necessarily criminal acts, as such. The security system operates outside the rules of the legal system and ideally ought not to be subject to judicial review—or, where unavoidable, such review should only take place within strict limits. This is compounded by the requirement that the security agency protect the identity of its sources, its modus operandi, and the content of its files from external publicity, and even from other sectors within the administrative apparatus of the state. In this way, the security apparatus takes on more or less of the attributes of a secret state within the state. The specific criteria for establishing risk will vary from regime to regime and from time to time, but in all times and all places these criteria will be overtly political, indicating borders between legitimate and illegitimate or safe and dangerous political opinions, associations, or expressions; less overtly, they may also encompass character "weaknesses" that are thought likely to make an individual vulnerable to blackmail or manipulation by hostile elements, but such "weaknesses" will usually themselves reflect political judgments about behavioral traits, such as condemnation of homosexuality or disapproval of lifestyles, and the like.

There were structural similarities between Hoover's FBI and Beria's KGB, however different in practice these two regimes and their secret police establishments. The point is not to offer moral equations, which would be inherently inappropriate, but rather to note how vastly different regimes, based on radically different principles, could nevertheless have followed certain structural paths that seem at least superficially similar. People who fell foul of the FBI might experience career problems, they might even lose their jobs and find themselves on a blacklist; very occasionally they might end up in prison or tied up in litigation. The victims of the Soviet secret police's displeasure were more likely to end in the gulag or dead. Yet in both cases human beings had become files, cases, shadow profiles of themselves that were more or less caricatures, bureaucratic cartoons that abstracted certain attributes, or alleged attributes, and exaggerated them: *X once associated with Y, who associated with known Trotskyites (Communists); infected by Trotskyism (Communism), X's subsequent behavior and thoughts must be reinterpreted as those of a subversive (counter)revolutionary.* Words and deeds that might otherwise seem innocent or unexceptional could take on the most sinister connotations, once the persona of the files began to overshadow the real-world individual. And these connotations could have real consequences for real people, more brutal in some regimes than in others, but in all cases based on the information amassed in the files of the political police.

THE LIBERAL INTELLIGENCE STATE

To see how this process operated, and still operates, in liberal democracies, we can turn to security screening in Western governments. Initially instituted ostensibly as a counterespionage measure to reduce the risk to governments of hiring public servants who might betray the trust placed in them, security screening has always and in all places taken on a life and momentum of its own, entailing complex security classifications of internal government information and thus of government jobs according to degrees of access to classified information. It has invariably resulted in the growth of a specialized bureaucracy-within-the-bureaucracy to administer the screening process, along with a body of specialized knowledge and screening techniques. A range of sanctions must be developed to deal with those who fail the screening tests, and—as we are speaking of liberal democracies—appeals procedures and mechanisms for administrative and judicial review must be established. However, in light of the nature of the evidence (concerning risk, not culpability) and in light of the imperative of security agencies to protect their sources and methods, independent review of the quality of information and of the interpretation put on the assembled evidence invariably proves to be a tricky and limited process.

A particularly striking feature of security screening is that while it promises an objective, rational technology of risk identification, on the analogy to medical screening (such as screening for the presence of tuberculosis or the HIV virus), it is in practice the very opposite of scientific risk identification. Set in motion to guard the state against hostile political ideologies, screening criteria are themselves hopelessly ideological. Thus the ravages of McCarthyism, using the term generically, throughout the Cold War. Worse, the ideological criteria have been extended to encompass behaviors deemed unseemly or abhorrent by conventional standards: "security" criteria were used to carry out vicious purges of gays and lesbians. And not content to confine screening to public servants alone, the process was extended in most Western countries to employees in "defense-related" industries and more recently, to positions considered vulnerable to terrorism (airport security, for instance). Most widely, it was extended in the early years of the Cold War to screen applicants for immigration and citizenship, and refugee claimants.

Two points should help explain the persistence and tenacity of security screening, which has easily outlived the Cold War. First, screening or something like it would have been an inevitability whatever the international climate. Modern states had to find ways to adapt to the conditions of mass democracy. There was a time when states could hire their public servants from small, closely integrated elites on the basis of personal trust. In class-dominated societies such as Britain, the tradition of drawing the administrative elite from the Oxbridge-educated upper classes persisted well into this century, but after the shocking dereliction of both class and nation by the so-called Cambridge ring of upper-class spies (Philby, Burgess, Maclean, Blunt and Cairncross) peculiarly drawn to the cause of proletarian revolution, it was apparent that the old-boy system of recruitment would no longer do—in the 1950s, "positive vetting" was established for sensitive positions in the British civil service. In the era of mass democracy, some appropriate alternative had to be found to the outmoded workings of familial and class trust. Not surprisingly, the alternative turned out to be the kind of abstract administrative mechanism, based on general universal categories, that any student of Weberian bureaucracy would have predicted. Yet it is doubtful that system more attuned to individual idiosyncrasies, or more tolerant of deviations from the political norm, could have been devised to deal with the problem of staffing large impersonal bureaucracies to administer large mass democracies.

Second, the need for security screening was not conjured from nothing. There was real espionage. States spy on each other, and states try to protect themselves from the prying eyes of their rivals. Hence the national insecurity state and its secret dossiers and data banks on the politics and beliefs of its citizens. The development of political policing of democracies was intimately related to the requirements of counterintelligence.

Not all the targets of the screening for spies and subversives were innocent. But the indictment of the security mania as "witch-hunting" has a large grain of truth in it. Many of the victims were guilty of no more than being on the wrong side of changing political fashions, of having once held what were now unpopular opinions, or simply of associating with or even being related to the wrong kind of persons. But to the screeners, "innocence" was beside the point. They were engaged in the great twentieth-century game of risk identification, the triage of separating the risky from the safe on the basis of the best information available from all sources, and thus securing the state from unnecessary hazards. Of course, it was possible that mistakes could be made, that information might prove faulty in some particulars, that innocence might be mistaken for something else. What was at stake was not legal guilt of an individual but simply risk from the point of view of the state. If any doubt existed as to the reliability or loyalty of an individual, the maxim went, such doubts should be resolved in favor of the state. A government job, immigration entry or citizenship were privileges, not rights. Anyway, there was little or no interest in individuals, as such. Individuals were *messy*, unfathomable in their complexity and idiosyncrasy to bureaucrats who had to deal with large numbers of cases and in universal categories. Dossiers were *neat*, simple and serviceable for the specific purposes required. The security forces gathered the data from sources that in many instances would not, for security reasons, bear cross-examination, and then the files were interpreted according to relatively straightforward criteria. If subjects tested as risky, then they *were* risks—by definition.

Owen Lattimore was a noted China scholar who taught at Johns Hopkins University. In 1950, he was named by Senator Joe McCarthy as the top Soviet spy in America. This bizarre charge, backed behind the scenes by Hoover's FBI, precipitated what Lattimore later called an "ordeal by slander," culminating in a perjury case against Lattimore that was finally called off in 1955 for total lack of evidence. In his account of the affair, Lattimore noted that the FBI and other agencies of the U.S. government and Congress had built up on him a dossier of a *"man who might have existed."*[22] That phrase catches the very essence of the creations of the national insecurity state: a data world that shadows, mimics, and caricatures the real world. Somewhere around mid-century in Western democracies, the data profiles of people who might have existed began to overshadow the people who actually did exist, a situation already in place in totalitarian police states for some time. This development was pioneered by the state sector, although, as we shall see later in this book, the private sector has since furthered and intensified the process, while subtly transforming its significance.

CITY OF GLASS: THE TOTALITARIAN INTELLIGENCE STATE

The twentieth century has been haunted by utopian dreams turned into dystopian nightmares. The dream of revolution entailed humanity remaking itself, translating a democratic ideal into material reality, realizing an ideological vision of social, economic, and cultural transformation. The dream of counterrevolution entailed racial purification and the triumph of the will of the *Volk*. The reality of both projects has been the totalitarian state, Stalinism and the *Führer-prinzip*, the gulag and Auschwitz. Today, at the end of the century, when we live amid the ruins of failed revolutions and

soured dreams, when the grand narratives that inspired and terror-
ized earlier generations have lost their hold and stuttered into inco-
herence, this story of utopia become dystopia no longer excites
more than the odd shrug or weary sigh. But it informs profoundly
our understanding of the relationship between power and knowledge.

The totalitarian state has existed in concrete forms, as a terrible
reality to those who have been ground under by its relentless machinery of repression. Yet it exists most memorably as a dream, or
nightmare, an ideal totalitarian state that stands above all the actual
such states as the Platonic geometric form stands above and beyond
all the actual imperfect material geometric shapes, but which is nevertheless implicit within them. The real Nazi Germany was an imperfect, sometimes chaotic, realization of Adolf Hitler's imagining,
but it is the *idea* of such a machinery of death that haunts us long
after the end of the regime and the end of the Nazi leaders. Stalinist
Russia in practice was a mass of contradictions, many of which still
remain to be sorted out by historians, yet the *concept* of a state driven
by the idea of a proletarian revolution harnessed to a monstrous cult
of personality, unbound by constraints of law or human rights, continues to grip the imagination even after that state eventually col-
lapsed under its own dead weight.

Perhaps this disjuncture between ideal and reality explains why
it is in the literary imagination of the Western world that the totalitarian state has been most vivid. George Orwell's *1984* is the para-
digmatic rendering of the totalitarian dystopia, whose basic
structure (a totalitarian future in which a one-party state police state
enforces its power by breaking its subjects' humanity) has informed
numerous imitations in popular culture. Orwell's novel was published at the outset of the Cold War and welcomed by the right-wing
media as a useful warning of the Communist threat to Western civilization.[23] Orwell himself borrowed the underlying structure of
1984 from a remarkable, but less-known Soviet dystopian novel,
Eugene Zamiatin's *We*,[24] written in 1920 in the immediate wake of
the Bolshevik Revolution and well before Stalin's seizure of power.
Zamiatin's work is more challenging than Orwell's because he

writes through the eyes of people already transformed by collectivism into a group consciousness that neither approves nor even understands individualism. But what is interesting in both writers is the architecture of totalitarianism they describe, and the chord this strikes in their readers.

In both novels, power is centralized in the one-party state, which ruthlessly crushes all dissent and allows for no opposition. Power is indeed ultimately personalized: Zamiatin's United State is presided over by the "Well-Doer," Orwell's Oceana by "Big Brother." Power is maintained through *surveillance*, minute and precise, of all subjects, or units of the collective ("Numbers" in Zamiatin). Nothing that anybody does, anywhere, escapes the ever-watchful eye of Big Brother/Well-Doer, while the messages of the party and leader are constantly beamed to the subjects through mass media; communication is thus one-way, hierarchical, and controlling. Subjects are constantly being trained and disciplined, yet this is hidden for the most part as the routinized, largely invisible fabric of everyday life. In Zamiatin, this is strikingly illustrated by the architecture within which people live and work: the city of the future is a *city of glass*, with everyone's lives transparent to everyone else—except of course those of the Well-Doer and the Guardians of the United State. The city is glass, but it is one-way glass.

Real-life totalitarian states never perfected Thought Control and were grossly inept at the everyday, seamless exercise of power through consent. Instead of leaving terror to the last resort of Orwell's "Room 101," where Winston Smith's resistance was finally crushed through terror, they fell back on terror as their first resort and were stained from head to toe with the blood of their victims. Rather than devilishly clever engineers of consent, they were mere clumsy butchers. Yet the image of the "ideal" totalitarian state remains vivid and compelling, and impossible to shake completely from our minds. I think this is because it is a kind of dark parable of what we have understood power to be. This parable is worth pausing over for a moment or two longer, as a signpost of where we have been in this century.

The totalitarian vision is so compelling because it represents the architectural skeleton of modern power. We have understood power as an amalgam of force and authority, exercized hierarchically, from the top down, centered in a commanding location above the society, and of which the people, or the civil society, are subjects but also instruments. To the extent that liberal democratic states have aped some of the features of this totalitarian vision—by establishing and empowering secret police and the apparatus of domestic Intelligence, however encumbered with constitutional constraints and notions of individual rights; by seeking to control or at least manage information in the interests of state security; by mobilizing knowledge in the service of power—we have caught glimpses in the totalitarian vision of ourselves, and not just of our enemies. To preserve the free society from its totalitarian antagonists, J. Edgar Hoover aspired to quasi-totalitarian power. Thus the peculiar mixture of fear and obsequious deference accorded Hoover in his lifetime, followed by revulsion and repudiation later, once he was safely in his grave. At an instinctive level, we knew and recognized Hoover as a totalitarian, which explains both the deference and the revulsion.

This nightmarish representation of power has haunted the twentieth century. It is sweeping and magnificent in its power to transfix the political imagination. *But it is almost certainly mistaken.* It no longer fits the realities of the world at the end of the twentieth century. Deep changes, technological, economic, cultural (some, but by no means all of which can be assembled under the umbrella of the so-called Information Revolution) have rendered this vision radically misleading. We need new representations of power that more accurately reflect and explain the contemporary world. What I attempt to do in the following chapters is to try to understand and explain some of these changes and how they might begin to add up to a more accurate representation of power. In the broadest brush strokes, what I am describing is the transition from the *surveillance state* to the *surveillance society*. This distinction is no mere formality. The surveillance society represents a very different complex of power, impacting in very different ways on authority, culture, society and politics, than did the state-centerd surveillance power of the immediate past.

NOTES TO CHAPTER 1

1. Numbers 13:1–2.
2. Michael J. Barrett, quoted in the frontispiece to Phillip Knightley, *The Second Oldest Profession: The Spy as Patriot, Bureaucrat, Fantasist and Whore* (London: Pan Books, 1987).
3. John Keegan, *The Second World War* (London: Penguin, 1989), 501.
4. Quoted in Ronald Radosh and Joyce Milton, *The Rosenberg File: A Search for the Truth* (N.Y.: Holt Rinehart & Winston, 1983), 284.
5. Andrew Hodges, *Alan Turing: The Enigma* (N.Y.: Simon & Schuster, 1983).
6. Robin W. Winks, *Cloak & Gown: Scholars in the Secret War, 1939–1961* (N.Y.: William Morrow & Co., 1987); Barry M. Katz, *Foreign Intelligence: Research and Analysis in the Office of Strategic Services, 1942–1945* (Cambridge, Mass.: Harvard University Press, 1989).
7. Michael Howard, *Strategic Deception in the Second World War* (London: Pimlico, 1992), ix.
8. J.C. Masterman, *The Double-Cross System in the War of 1939 to 1945* (Yale University Press, 1972).
9. Mary Kaldor, *The Imaginary War: Understanding the East-West Conflict* (Oxford: Blackwell, 1990).
10. Tom Mangold, *Cold Warrior: James Jesus Angleton, the CIA's Master Spy Hunter* (London: Simon & Schuster, 1991).
11. Peter Wright, *Spycatcher: The Candid Autobiography of a Senior Intelligence Officer* (Toronto: Stoddard Publishing, 1987).
12. David E. Murphy, Sergei A. Kondrashev, and George Bailey, *Battlefield Berlin: CIA vs. KGB in the Cold War* (New Haven: Yale University Press, 1997). This account is co-authored by two of the principal antagonists in the Berlin Intelligence wars.
13. Seymour M. Hersh, *"The Target is Destroyed": What Really Happened to Flight 007 and What America Knew About It* (N.Y.: Random House, 1986).
14. Michael R. Beschloss, *Mayday: Eisenhower, Khrushchev and the U-2 Affair* (N.Y.: Harper & Row, 1986).
15. Jeffrey T. Richelson, *The US Intelligence Community* (Cambridge, Mass.: Ballinger, 1985) 107–17; William E. Burrows, *Deep Black: Space Espionage and National Security* (N.Y.: Random House, 1986).
16. Walter Pincus, "Smaller Spy Satellites May Give U.S. Stealth Capability Over Trouble Spots," *Washington Post*, Feb. 1, 1998.
17. Jeffrey T. Richelson, "Scientists in Black," *Scientific American* (Feb. 1998) 48–55.
18. David Stafford, *The Silent Game: The Real World of Imaginary Spies* (Toronto: Lester & Orpen Dennys, 1988).
19. Christopher Andrew, *Secret Service: The Making of the British Intelligence Community* (London: Sceptre, 1986), 100.
20. John J. Dziak, *Chekisty: A History of the KGB* (Lexington, Mass.: D.C. Heath & Co., 1988).
21. Timothy Garton Ash, *The File: A Personal History* (N.Y.: Random House, 1997).
22. Owen Lattimore, *Ordeal by Slander* (Boston: Little, Brown, 1950). For a more recent study of this affair, based on declassified FBI documents, see Robert P. Newman,

Owen Lattimore and the 'Loss' of China (Berkeley: University of California Press, 1992).

23. George Orwell, *1984* (London: Martin Secker & Warburg, 1949).

24. Unpublishable in the U.S.S.R. itself due to censorship, *We* was circulated in proto-*zamizdat* form. It was first published in English in 1924 and reprinted again in 1952 at the height of the Cold War, perhaps as a nod to the success of *1984*: Eugene Zamiatin, *We* (translated by Gregory Zilboorg, N.Y.: E.P. Dutton & Co., 1924 and 1952).

2—The Panopticon

In any discussion of the organized Intelligence capacity of the state, both for internal and external purposes, surveillance is a key concept. But what exactly do we mean by surveillance, and to what uses has it been put? According to Christopher Dandeker, one of the leading theorists on the subject:

> The exercise of surveillance involves one or more of the following activities: (1) the collection and storage of information (presumed to be useful) about people or objects; (2) the supervision of the activities of people or objects through the issuing of instructions or the physical design of the natural and built environments. In this context, architecture is of significance for the supervision of people—as for instance in prison and urban design; (3) the application of information gathering activities to the business of monitoring the behaviour of those under supervision, and, in the case of subject persons, their compliance with instructions.[1]

THE PANOPTICON

The image of the Panopticon permeates all contemporary discussions of surveillance. The word and the idea were coined by the English utilitarian philosopher Jeremy Bentham in 1787[2]. Taken up by the late French philosopher Michel Foucault in the 1970s[3], the concept remains influential. When Oscar H. Gandy, Jr., set out in the 1990s to discuss the implications of the latest information technologies for a "political economy of personal information," he titled his book *The Panoptic Sort*.[4]

The Panopticon was in fact a proposed architectural design by Bentham for a prison. The idea of the Panopticon is simple. Imagine a prison constructed in a circular form. On the outer perimeter of each level are the individual cells, each housing a single prisoner and each entirely isolated from the other to make it impossible for a prisoner to see or hear fellow prisoners. Each cell is visible to the gaze of the Inspector, who is housed in a central office from which he can scan all cells on the same level. Through a system of apertures and communication tubes too complicated to describe here (and in practice probably too complicated to construct) each prisoner is aware of the potential scrutiny of the Inspector at any time of the day or night (light floods the cells naturally by day and artificially by night), and prisoners receive verbal communications from the Inspector from time to time through "conversation tubes" that carry his personalized instructions which cannot be overheard by prisoners for whom they are not intended. Although the prisoners' behavior is made permanently visible to the Inspector, the prisoners cannot actually see the face and eyes of the Inspector who, again through a complicated arrangement of lanterns and apertures, is rendered opaque, a silhouette that reminds them of his continuous presence, but an "utterly dark spot" whose features cannot be deciphered.

The Panopticon is a kind of theatre; what is staged is "the illusion of constant surveillance: the prisoners are not really always under surveillance, they just think or imagine that they are."[5] The point is *discipline* or *training*. As the prisoners fear that they may be constantly watched, and fear punishment for transgressions, they internalize the rules; actual punishment will thus be rendered superfluous. In another sense, the entire Panopticon is itself a kind of theatrical spectacle for the benefit of the public, members of which will be invited to observe (Bentham was a great believer in the exemplary value of publicity). Reformation of the prisoners themselves is almost of secondary interest. The wider purpose is the moral reformation of the society through the edifying spectacle of discipline via surveillance. And Bentham further specified that the principle of the Panopticon could and should be extended to various bounded sites of human activity, from asylums to the eighteenth-century equivalent of welfare institutions, to workplaces, to schools.

The design was never realized, either in Bentham's own lifetime or since. Yet as a metaphor of the power of surveillance in the contemporary world, it is unparalleled. To Foucault, Bentham's idea was that of a "political technology" that induces in the subject "a state of conscious and permanent visibility that assures the automatic functioning of power."[6] The imaginary totalitarian state of 1984 has transfixed the political imagination as a glimpse of the skeletal architecture of state power. The imaginary Panopticon equally transfixes as a glimpse into the otherwise silent, invisible workings of the technique of power internalized, of power exercised without the direct presence of coercion.

Bentham, typically, was not backward in his claims for his concept. The man who was described by Karl Marx as the "the arch-Philistine, that insipid, pedantic, leather-tongued oracle of the ordinary bourgeois intelligence of the 19th century"[7] could barely contain his excitement in the first words in his preface to his *Panopticon*: "Morals reformed—health preserved—industry invigorated—instruction diffused—public burthens lightened—Economy seated, as it were, upon a rock—the Gordian knot of the Poor-laws are not cut, but untied—all by a simple idea in Architecture!" Bentham goes on to elaborate "the whole of the way before me" as "a new mode of obtaining power of mind over mind, in a quantity hitherto without example . . . Such is the engine: such is the work that may be done with it."[8] This "engine" is based upon what seems indeed to be a simple idea of architectural construction, but it is by no means as simple as Bentham claimed. The practical complexity of working out the simple idea proved too great to commend the plan to anyone charged with actually building and running a prison, but it is the richness of the concept and its deep resonance in modernity that give it lasting importance. Bentham thought of himself as a practical reformer, armed with blueprints for concrete projects. Ironically, this dour social engineer, the very embodiment of Edmund Burke's warning of the coming age of "sophisters, economists and calculators," had in the case of the Panopticon hit not on a practical blueprint but rather a brilliant metaphor for power in modern societies.

Bentham's messianic sense of his project's social mission is underlined by his insistence on the place of religious worship and instruction in his penitentiary, but even more strikingly by the underlying parallels between the Panopticon and the idea of an invisible but all-seeing, all-powerful God. The Inspector *sees without being seen*. His presence, which is also an absence, is in his gaze alone. The prisoners, incarcerated in their individual cells, are also incarcerated in their bodies. They cannot escape the sweeping gaze that seems to stand outside the corporeal world, yet penetrates it and renders it transparent. Of course, the omnipresence of the Inspector is nothing more than an architectural artifice, really just an elaborate conjuring trick. There is a real Inspector (Bentham, ever practical, even discusses arrangements for the housing of his family), but he disappears into the "utterly dark spot" that the prisoners witness. It is the imaginary Inspector, this by-product of architectural construction, who overshadows mundane reality. Thus the relation between the idea of God and the Church on earth.

The religious parallel runs deeper yet. God is hidden yet omnipresent, as in the New Testament. Nevertheless, like the Old Testament God, he intervenes strategically to ensure that his presence is acknowledged. For instance, Bentham suggests that small infractions by prisoners might be left apparently unnoticed for a few days, thus emboldening them to attempt larger transgressions. Finally the Voice lists an inventory of past infractions, and prisoners henceforth become aware that impunity is an illusion, that even silence on the part of the Inspector means only that he has chosen, for mysterious reasons of his own, not to intervene yet. God/Inspector knows all, but is himself unknowable.

The Panopticon is, at bottom, nothing more than sleight of hand. But according to Bentham it creates a context in which the subjects have no alternative but to believe that appearance is reality. The key is surveillance. The Panopticon is, like Oceana and the United State, a city of one-way glass. But herein lies a problem, of which Bentham appears to have been blissfully unaware. Bentham believed that surveillance would ensure compliance, without the need for coercion. Prisoners would become docile through constant training, as rules became internalized and consent replaced mere obedience. Yet compliance ultimately rests on the threat of coercion. Moreover, the very reason the subjects of the Panopticon are there to be watched and trained is because they are prisoners deprived of civil liberty and personal choice. All the institutions to which Bentham believed his panoptic principle could be applied were similarly based on degrees of coercion.

If the conjuring trick of surveillance to produce consent requires actual or threatened coercion, is there not a paradox at the heart of the panoptic project? Perfect consent will only be achieved by the prior perfection of coercion. Otherwise, why would the subjects remain under the Inspector's gaze? Why, if they are not forcibly confined, will they allow the Inspector to remain an "utterly dark spot," knowing yet unknowable? What will prevent them from breaking the one-way glass and finding, like Dorothy and her companions, the insecure, unprepossessing little man manipulating and hiding behind the intimidating public face of the Wizard of Oz?

Religion has tried to deal with this problem of moral enforcement by positing a God who exacts punishment or provides rewards in the afterlife. However, this has always been a less than satisfactory way of ensuring compliance with the moral code in the present life, especially when the material rewards of ignoring or shortcutting God's moral precepts may be more immediately compelling. But for the logic of panopticism, there is no afterlife as sanction, only the here and now. Bentham's metaphor shows how surveillance can exact compliance and thus be an effective tool for social control, but only to the extent that the subjects of surveillance have no alternative to submitting themselves to the Inspector's gaze. The history of surveillance in the Western world in the nineteenth and twentieth centuries both conforms to the Benthamite logic of panopticism and persistently departs from it. The logic is compelling, and social and political analysts have pointed to very important insights encoded within the panoptic design. But the subjects of panoptic control have often resisted. The Panopticon has therefore been a contested concept, and that is how I treat it in this book.

A SHORT HISTORY OF SURVEILLANCE

In his ground-breaking work on the birth of the prison, Foucault was attracted to the concept of panopticism for "the imaginary intensity that it has possessed for almost two hundred years":

> But the Panopticon must not be understood as a dream building: it is the diagram of a mechanism of power reduced to its ideal form; its functioning, abstracted from any obstacle, resistance or friction, must be represented as a pure architectural and optical system: it is in fact a figure of political technology that may and must be detached from any specific use.[9]

Although Foucault addressed himself specifically to prisons, and in an earlier book to asylums,[10] he noted that the principles of panopticism should not be limited to such enclosures, deliberately isolated and detached from society. The disciplines organized in enclosed places — barracks, schools, workshops — "Bentham dreamt of transforming into a network of mechanisms that would be everywhere and always alert, running through society without interruption in space or in time." Thus Foucault saw in the eighteenth and nineteenth centuries a "movement of exceptional discipline to one of a generalized surveillance . . . the gradual extension of the mechanisms of discipline . . . their spread throughout the whole social body, the formation of what might be called in general the disciplinary society."[11] The panoptic technology spread from specialized, enclosed institutions to the administrative authorities that organized these institutions, and finally to "state apparatuses whose major, if not exclusive, function is to assure that discipline reigns over society as a whole [the police]."

> One can speak of the formation of a disciplinary society in this movement that stretches from the enclosed disciplines, a sort of social "quarantine," to an indefinitely generalizable mechanism of "panopticism." Not because the disciplinary modality of power has replaced all the others; but because it has infiltrated all the others, sometimes undermining them, but serving as an intermediary between them, linking them together, extending them and making it possible to bring the effects of power to the most minute and distant elements. It assures an infinitesimal distribution of the power relations.[12]

THE PANOPTIC FACTORY

As the British social theorist Anthony Giddens makes clear, the development of the modern nation-state is bound up with the growth of surveillance as a crucial mechanism of administrative control.[13] But the predominant form of the modern state has not only been as *nation*-state but as *capitalist* state. Capitalism separates the economic from the political and creates the distinct, although interrelated, compartments of the private sector and the public sector. If, as Foucault suggests, panoptic principles spread through infiltration, the capitalist workplace ought to be a good place to begin to look for them.

Knowledge is a productive resource, and nowhere has this been more evident than in the organization of the capitalist workplace. Adam Smith famously showed the productive power of the division of labor with his description of how a pin factory vastly outproduced a pin-maker by dividing the process of pin-making into eighteen distinct operations, each performed by different workers.[14] These operations and these workers have to be organized and monitored on a permanent basis. Following the Industrial Revolution, the factory became a primary site for innovation in forms of surveillance and discipline, driven by market pressures to enhance efficiency and economy in the productive process. With the advent of the assembly line, workers were inserted into a constant mechanized flow of production in which they became in effect as interchangeable as the parts they were assembling. On the assembly line, a worker's every action was automatically recorded in the continuity of the flow—and every deviation instantly noted in the interruption of the process. The great impresario of the mass-production assembly line, Henry Ford, did not rest content with the surveillance/control over his workers allowed by the factory itself. Notoriously, he expected workers' "private" lives to conform to his managerial expectations of moral probity, and sent out company spies (organized, significantly, in what the Ford company called its "Sociology Department") to police workers' behavior in their "off" hours. With the challenge of trade unions, capitalist surveillance of the workplace assumed more aggressive policing functions. Management developed for its own purposes some of the security and intelligence capacities typical of the modern national security state, to prevent the infiltration of union organizers past the factory gates in the first instance, and when that failed, to closely watch union activities and to counter and undermine strikes.

The capitalist workplace had its own Bentham, a theorist of the panoptic factory. Frederick Winslow Taylor in the early twentieth century developed and promoted "scientific management," not merely as a managerial plan of action for the workplace, but as a panacea for the more efficient functioning of every aspect of capitalist society. Like Bentham, Taylor thought of himself essentially as a practical man (he invented a process of high-speed steel production) rather than a dreamer, yet like Bentham he is remembered more for a theoretical ideal—one that in fact bears his name as an ideology: "Taylorism."[5] The essence of Taylorism, or scientific management, was to apply the same principle of the division of labor enunciated by Adam Smith for the factory as a form of productive organization to the individual labor process. According to Taylor, all work could be broken down into distinct motions, and greater efficiency could be effected by scientific analysis of these motions to discover the "one best way" of doing each job. Time and motion studies by Taylor and his disciples brought to the factory floor the figure of the efficiency expert armed with stopwatch and clipboard. Management, wreathed in an aura of science, now claimed a monopoly of useful knowledge about the labor process, in effect appropriating the worker's craft and reducing him or her to a unit whose functioning would be controlled by minute and continuous observation. In the panoptic workplace, the Inspector was replaced by the efficiency expert, but the result was much the same: subjects were controlled by the unblinking gaze of the all-knowing but unknowable watcher. A system of piece-rate compensation geared to precisely measured productivity would ensure that compliance and performance were exacted without recourse to overt coercive power.

Or so the theory went. Like Bentham's Panopticon, Taylor's system, *qua* system, was more memorable as a construct of the imagination than as concrete reality—not least because of resistance from workers unwilling to serve merely as speeded-up work-machines to increase the owners' profits. Once again, panoptic dreams falter on the limitations of the underlying coercive power necessary to make the system of seemingly voluntary compliance actually work. In the event, the early pristine form of scientific management theory was followed by "human relations" schools of management thought that emphasized more conciliatory (critics would say more deceptive) methods of enlisting employees' consensual agreement to participate in the managerial plan. Yet even if Taylorism as an ideology has fallen from fashion, scientific management has endured: power in the workplace rests not only on the ownership of capital and the appropriation of the workers' labor power (the background, structural condition) but in everyday operational terms on management's superior surveillance capacity and the concentration of useful knowledge that capacity yields. Worker resistance has impeded the untrammelled exercise of that power but it has never succeeded in reversing it.

Surveillance as workplace control is particularly effective because it is *reflexive*. "Management" not only monitors workers, it monitors itself. Efficiency studies have been as much about administrative and supervisory processes as about production. As we shall see later in this book, the diffusion of new information technologies in the workplace has not only greatly enhanced the power of disciplinary surveillance over what was once called the "shop floor," but has also intensified the reflexive capacity of management to monitor its own performance and to take appropriate measures to improve its efficiency. Indeed, the new technologies even permit the displacement of the traditional workplace and the geographic dispersal of both workers and management, with no diminution of supervisory surveillance over their activities: the Panopticon decentered.

THE PANOPTIC STATE

Capitalist enterprise, in short, has been and continues to be a primary site not only for the exercise of surveillance, but also a site for technological and organizational innovations in surveillance. At the same time, the history of capitalism has, until recently at least, been the history of national capitalisms, where nation-states have acted as containers — leaky containers, it is true, but containers nonetheless. The modern nation-state involves the extension of sovereignty as the monopoly of the legitimate exercise of coercion over a given territory, most often, although not always coterminous with the hegemony of a single language, culture, and national identity. The modern state has been an administrative unit, organizing the national territory, setting and enforcing rules, maintaining law and order, adjudicating disputes over resource allocation, redistributing resources through taxation and expenditures, and providing the social and economic infrastructure for capitalist enterprise. Because no state has been an island onto itself, states have also had to provide for commercial, diplomatic and military relations with other states, which has meant in practice the mounting of professional standing armies and the economic, technological capacity and will to wage war on the modern scale.

All of this has required knowledge and especially reflexive knowledge—that is, the increased capacity of the state to monitor itself and its activities. To tax its citizens, it must know the distribution of property and income, and it must also control its own means of raising revenues. Before the emergence of the modern state, taxation was farmed out, a practice that not only led to widespread corruption and oppression, but also diffused power and weakened the central state. Centralized taxation requires a centralized information base: the state must know what is available to be taxed and from whom it is to be extracted; in gathering and analyzing this information, the state also gains an appreciation of itself, its own fiscal capacities and limitations. Similarly, in rule enforcement and policing, the state gathers intelligence on citizens, organizations, groups, and classes through various means, and acts on this information in strategic interventions in the civil society, as well as in the day-to-day maintenance of order. By the same process, the state also monitors its own legitimacy and authority.

In all these typical state activities, surveillance is a crucial tool. Indeed, in a very deep sense, it is the most crucial tool of all. Much that is quite specific to the modern state we take for granted, so much so as to fail to appreciate its uniqueness in broader historical perspective. For instance, the routine gathering of statistics covering every aspect of society, culture, and economy is an activity intrinsic to the modern state, but one that barely existed in anything but the most rudimentary and fragmentary form in earlier eras. The gathering of social statistics permits an historically unprecedented degree of collective self-consciousness. Society has become an object of its own reflection, but in a way that mirrors the statistical method: quantitative relationships crowd out qualitative; categories, classes and other "objective" constructs crowd out human beings. The object is always to construct an understanding of the social world in order to change or control it. Statistical information is ideal for providing "handles" on subjects. The inner moral qualities of individuals are not measurable; their productive activities, their property holdings, their disposable income, their expenditures, their contractual relationships, their infractions of the law, are all measurable and provide opportunities for regulation. The inner life of individuals (their thoughts and motives) is not calculable, but behavior can be monitored and recorded. Statistical surveillance is never knowledge for its own sake, never philosophy (literally: love of knowledge). It is always knowledge for the sake of control, and it has most often been in the service of the state — although, as we shall see later, perhaps less so in the present and near future than in the immediate past.

The social sciences, sometimes called the "behavioral" sciences, emerged simultaneously with the emergence of the knowledgeable state. This is no accident, any more than the dependence of the social sciences on the statistics gathered by the state is merely coincidental. The very conceptualizations of "society" by sociologists, "economy" by economists, and "government" by political scientists have been structured by the kind of statistics that states felt required to gather and how they organized the information. And then, to close the circle, social scientists have in turn helped shape the state's statistical profiles by the enrichment and elaboration of these conceptualizations. This symbiotic relationship — of which the odd-couple relationship of spy and scholar, discussed in the last chapter, forms a subset — is a product of the reflexive knowledge made possible by the modern state form. Nor can it be separated from the will to power inherent in this capacity to broaden and deepen collective self-consciousness of the kind described. Whether as political projects launched for state action or as social science schools of interpretation, knowledge is not analytically distinct from the control that knowledge promises. This remains true whether the motive is one of reform or of conservatism; changing or reproducing the social order are both problems of manipulation, intervention, and control. Both require a statistical base.

From the point of view of the surveillance state, a crucial development is a rational administrative apparatus, a modern bureaucracy, as Max Weber used the term.[16] Bureaucrats are appointed and promoted on merit, not on the basis of kinship or patronage: it is the office and function, not the person and his or her connections, that is all-important. Administration must take place within a context of settled rules, with expectations of a reasonable degree of predictability. Compliance with administrative regulations and commands is normal, routinized. For this system to be maintained, information is key. The ability of the administrative state to administer rests on its extensive knowledge about the society and the knowledge of where and when deviations from compliance occur.

Within an efficient administrative state, panoptic power can be reproduced in various sites to watch different categories of people. Schools prepare people over a prolonged childhood, adolescent, and young-adult training period for the discipline of the workplace or office. The discipline of the workplace of course only applies to those who are employed; for those who are unemployed, unemployable, or retired, the state provides welfare or social security programs that are themselves elaborate surveillance systems that maintain detailed information on their clients. In every case there are powerful incentives (income or benefits) for remaining voluntarily under the panoptic gaze, and disincentives for evading the gaze. If, despite this array of carrots and sticks, deliberate evasion is practiced, there is a good possibility that the evader will end up subject to criminal sanction, which is to say, a prisoner in the narrower Benthamite sense.

Once again, we can see the primary principle of the Panopticon in operation. The Inspector, now the Bureaucrat, scans the subjects, now the Society, rendered as transparent as possible to his gaze. The transparency is not however two-way, as the state jealously guards itself through administrative secrecy. It appears to the subjects as an impenetrable object (and separated as administration is from politics, not directly accountable to democratic voters). Coercion lurks in the background, of course, as an underlying sanction encouraging compliance with a state which has a high likelihood of seeing and noting infractions of its rules. The difference between the panoptic state and Bentham's Panopticon is one of complexity. The society is a much vaster and infinitely more complicated phenomenon than a prison, less knowable and thus less controllable. Nor is there a Bureaucrat who can stand in for the Inspector, as such. The volume of information secured by the vast apparatus of state surveillance of the society is far too high for any individual to process and act on. That is precisely why a Weberian bureaucracy must accompany the surveillance state: its hierarchical ordering of offices and functions is supposed to facilitate the collective rational marshalling of information. The collective Inspector is in effect broken down into a functional division of labor to play essentially the same surveillance role, with essentially the same objective: internalization of the rules by the subject and compliance without overt coercion whenever possible.

The modern administrative state has been a great innovator of technologies and techniques of surveillance. The state's military apparatus generated much of this innovation[17] (as discussed with regard to Intelligence in the previous chapter.) Policing, where the coercive underpinning of state power is most visible, has also been in the vanguard of innovation. Other administrative arms of the state have developed techniques of gathering information specific to their particular concerns, such as health protection, a field in which advanced methods of health-related surveillance of large populations have originated from the state sector.

THE RISK-AVERSIVE PANOPTICON

The panoptic analogy would not be complete without one further, crucial extension. Bentham's Panopticon employed punitive sanctions against rule-breakers, but more importantly it exercised preventative control. The administrative state, joined by the corporate sector, goes a step further by establishing the statistical probability of the *risk* that categories of people will break the rules. When risk can be confidently calculated, potential rule-breakers can be excluded from the opportunity of noncompliance. Large organizations, whether public or private, engage constantly in risk analysis and exhibit risk-aversive behavior. Some observers have gone so far as to speak of a contemporary "risk society."[18] Certainly the web of data and the definitional framework relating to risk factors (what have been called "risk communication systems") are themselves leading panoptic elements. Risks must be managed and contained; prevention is always more cost-effective and less socially disruptive than after-the-fact punishment. The panoptic state is thus increasingly future-oriented and concerned about the predictive power of the information it gathers, just as the capitalist corporation is oriented toward the future return on its investment. Both become in effect hostages to uncertainty and eagerly, if not greedily, scan and store as much information as possible to reduce the level of uncertainty.

The informational appetite of risk aversion seems indefinitely expandable. With the new technologies of information gathering, processing, storage and retrieval, the panoptic tendencies in modern society gain immeasurably in scope and efficiency. I turn to these new technologies and their effects in the following chapters.

NOTES TO CHAPTER 2

1. Christopher Dandeker, *Surveillance, Power and Modernity: Bureaucracy and Discipline from 1700 to the Present Day* (N.Y.: St. Martin's Press, 1990), 37.

2. Jeremy Bentham, *The Panopticon Writings*, Miran Božovǐ, ed. (London: Verso, 1995).

3. Michel Foucault, *Surveiller et punir: naissance de la prison* (Paris: Gallimard, 1975); trans. Alan Sheridan, *Discipline and Punish: The Birth of the Prison* (N.Y.: Pantheon, 1978).

4. Oscar H. Gandy, Jr., *The Panoptic Sort: A Political Economy of Personal Information* (Boulder, Colo.: Westview Press, 1993).

5. Bentham, Introduction, 16.

6. Foucault, 207, 201 (references are to the English edition).

7. Karl Marx, *Capital*, (Londen: Lawrence & Wishpert 1972) v. 1: Part VII, ch. xxiv, s. 5.

8. Bentham, 31. The full title of the work gives some idea of the grandeur of Bentham's pretensions: "Panopticon; Or, the Inspection House: Containing the Idea of a New Principle of Construction Applicable to any Sort of Establishment, in Which Persons of any Description Are to Be Kept Under Inspection; And in Particular to Penitentiary-houses, Prisons, Houses of Industry, Work-houses, Poor-houses, Manufactories, Mad-houses, Lazarettos, Hospitals, and Schools With a Plan of Management Adapted to This Principle."

9. Foucault, 205.

10. Foucault, *Histoire de la folie à l'âge classique* (Paris: Collection 10/18, 1961); English edition, trans. Richard Howard, *Madness and Civilization* (N.Y.: Pantheon, 1965).

11. Foucault, *Discipline and Punish*, 209.

12. Ibid. 216.

13. Anthony Giddens, *The Nation-State and Violence* (Berkeley: University of California Press, 1987).
14. Adam Smith, *The Wealth of Nations* (1776, new ed., N.Y.: Random House, 1937), 4–5.
15. Reg Whitaker, 'Scientific management as political ideology', *Studies in Political Economy* 2 (1979), 75–108.
16. Max Weber, *The Theory of Social and Economic Organizations* (London: W. Hodge, 1947).
17. Dandeker, *Surveillance, Power and Modernity*, is particularly interesting on the military contribution to surveillance technology.
18. Richard V. Ericson and Kevin D. Haggerty, *Policing the Risk Society* (Toronto: University of Toronto Press, 1997).

3—Cyberspace: The Library of Babel[1]

Fin-de-siècle capitalist culture is awash with prophecies of revolution. We are told that we are in the process of a transformation so profound that we can barely discern its implications. But this time the spectre is not that of revolution from below, but from outside, through the miraculous agency of that deus ex machina, technology. The Agricultural Revolution and the Industrial Revolution are now to be surpassed by the Information Revolution. The computer is transforming economy, society, culture, human beings themselves.

To the prophets, the digital futurologists of capitalism, this revolution is no spectre, but a beacon pointing the way to a brighter future. The future will be entirely different from the present, yet *plus ça change, plus c'est la même chose:* capitalism will be engine of this transformation because it is capitalism that taps the wellsprings of technological change, capitalism that knows how to put technology to practical use, and capitalism that can market the new technologies. Some capitalists will be thrown off by the great wheel of *laissez innover,* but those who learn to ride it will be rewarded with positions on the commanding heights of the new world.[2]

Against this siren chorus of conservative revolutionaries there stands a smaller, less electronically articulate and less media literate but equally enthusiastic group of leftish prophets who see the seeds of social revolution in the new technologies. Democracy will spring not from the barrel of a gun but from the personal computer and modem. States and corporations will lose control over the flow of information. The People will rule the Internet.[3]

Both camps are united at least on the principle that technology is now the autonomous engine of history. It is as if some cosmic dice are being cast, and we await nervously, excitedly, to see the results. There is a third camp, not politically identifiable under traditional labels, that shares this technological determinism. But these are pessimists who think the results will be bad, destroying jobs, displacing values, degrading society, and stunting our culture.[4]

Finally, there is a fourth camp, also politically uncategorizable, that rejects the technological determinism of the others, derides the prevalent infohype, and argues that we can turn back the great wheel, or at least stop it in its tracks, if we recognize the flimsiness and pretense of the prophecies.[5] The Information Revolution is in this perspective simply an incremental change in the way we do things, not a qualitative leap into the unknown.

Given the breathless, up-to-the-minute quality of so much discussion of this question, it is something of a shock to discover that a perfect image of the Information Age was penned some forty years ago by an Argentinian writer innocent of any interest whatever in the technology of the present or the future. This is Jorge Luis Borges' remarkable vision of the "Library of Babel:"[6]

> The universe (which others call the Library) is composed of an indefinite and perhaps infinite number of hexagonal galleries. . . . From any of the hexagons one can see, interminably, the upper and lower floors. The distribution of the galleries is invariable. Twenty shelves, five long shelves per side, cover all the sides except two; their height, which is the distance from floor to ceiling, scarcely exceeds that of a normal bookcase. One of the free sides leads to a narrow hallway which opens into another gallery, identical to the first and to all the rest . . . Also through here passes a spiral stairway, which sinks abysmally and soars upward to remote distances. In the hallway there is a mirror which faithfully duplicates all appearances. . . . The Library is a sphere whose exact centre is any one of its hexagons and whose circumference is inaccessible.

The Library of Babel envisages the universe as a repository of information; life is the activity of retrieving and interpreting information. In the past, this vision might have been shrugged off as little more than the hallucination of a scholar mistaking his own crabbed, bibliophile existence with life itself. When the great eighteenth-century historian Edward Gibbon presented the second volume of his monumental *Decline and Fall of the Roman Empire* to the Duke of Gloucester, the Duke responded: "Another damned thick, square book! Always scribble, scribble, scribble, eh, Gibbon?" Has Borges the scribbler simply conjured up a metaphorical universe-as-library? No doubt. Yet that metaphor touches on something very deep indeed in the Information Age. We are all "scribblers" now, even if the scribbling is via keyboards rather than pens and pencils, and is stored less in "thick, square books" than in the ether of cyberspace. The promise of the Information Revolution is precisely that the key to the infinite Library will be in our hands, this Library "whose circumference is inaccessible" yet is a "sphere whose exact center is any one of its hexagons." We will once again be restored to the exact center of a universe we were long ago expelled from by science that decentered humanity. From this center we can command the sight lines of all the other hexagons stretching away in every direction, and reach out as far as we want in instantaneous real-time to retrieve the precise piece of information we want at any moment.

In the infinite (and infinitely centered) hexagons of the Library, it is not only writers and scholars who scan the shelves. It is business people organizing their enterprises, calling up marketing data, orchestrating outsourced production inputs, commanding financial and accountancy services, and systematizing the information inflow and outflow that will optimize their operations and maximize their profitability. It is generals and admirals running C^3I (command, control, communications, and intelligence/information) through a virtual battlefield on a computer screen. It is farmers organizing the care and cultivation of their fields according to the analysis of a computer program linked to digitalized imaging from a space satellite. It is a football coach sending in plays to his quarterback based on probabilities calculated by a program in a notebook computer on the sidelines. It is a taxi driver whose smart cab is computing the fastest route through the maze of metropolitan streets, instantly adjusted to take account of current traffic flows. The common thread linking all these different occupations and activities, and myriads of others as well, is information processing. Each requires skills, knowledge, and craft that cannot be detached entirely from the individual practitioners —*yet*. But to an extent never witnessed in any earlier age, more and more activities are being translated into information processing, then translated back again into action. This might seem an extra, if not unnecessary, step, but this mediation unlocks revolutionary new powers.

The intermediate step, the conversion of the material into manipulable abstract representation is in the universal language of digitization. Information is encoded in machine-readable form, which is to say, in a form reducible to combinations of the symbols 0 and 1, which represent high or low voltage, on or off switches. Digital encoding is a universal language in that any media of expression can be stored in digital form and then restored: text, sounds, images can all be transmuted into data and reconstituted at will. Moreover, the restoration is exact. Once something is digitally encoded, there is no longer anything that can be called an original as opposed to a copy. There is only one Mona Lisa; copies, however expertly done, remain only that. An image or text or piece of music produced in digital form can be reproduced multiple times with no degradation of its integrity whatsoever. Those receiving the object may "improve" it by adding to it or subtracting from it, without in any way compromising the integrity of the unedited version which will now coexist with multiple variations. Unlike the case of the art vandal who gouges an eye and paints a mustache on the Mona Lisa, thus damaging the original irreparably, digital objects can be altered or reproduced indefinitely: a one-eyed Mona Lisa with a mustache will coexist for the ages with a digitally untouched Mona Lisa (presuming others want to give the revised version immortality by reproducing it).

There is yet more to digitization. The Mona Lisa as a material object deteriorates, and requires elaborate climate- and light-controlled maintenance, even perhaps partial restoration from time to time to counteract the effects of aging. A digital Mona Lisa on the other hand does not "age" because the digital code that describes the object is an abstraction that stands, in a sense, outside of time.[7] And there is still more. The one-of-a-kind Mona Lisa painting is a material object that occupies a precise physical location in space: a particular wall in the Louvre gallery in Paris. When an arrangement was made a number of years ago for exhibiting the painting in New York, elaborate arrangements had to be made to transport the physical object to North America, to house and secure it while there, and then return it intact to its regular home. A digital Mona Lisa, on the other hand, may be transmitted more or less instantaneously from Paris to New York at extremely low cost compared to the physical transportation of the painting. In fact any number of exact replications of a digital Mona Lisa can coexist simultaneously with one another in any number of locations around the globe.

Digitization permits an astonishing alchemy: transportation (of physical objects) is transformed into communication (of information bits). This has staggering cost-reduction implications, leading to a new business imperative: ship bits, not boxes. For instance, there was once a time when readers of the *New York Times* outside New York had to await the arrival of the daily newspaper via trucks, trains, or airplanes. Then a digitized version was bounced off satellites to printing plants in various locations around the continent which then produce the paper for distribution in that area. But digitization permits an even more direct form of transmission. Now I can receive the *Times* on my computer screen, read what I choose to read off the screen, download articles of particular interest either in hard-copy form or for electronic storage and later reference or quotation, and redistribute articles to anyone with access to Internet sevices, anywhere, instantly. All this, it should be emphasized, is done in sovereign disregard of the once-formidable barriers erected by time and space. I can receive my daily newspaper in real time whether I am in Toronto or Tokyo.[8]

Digitization is a kind of alchemy, but there is nothing magic about it. The key is the universal language of 0s and 1s. That universality is unprecedented. Thus the renewed relevance and the promise of Borges' Library as a metaphor for the world.

FROM COLOSSUS TO MICROPROCESSOR: MAKING THE ALCHEMY WORK

The innovations that made digitization are basically two: smaller, faster, and smarter computers, and global real-time communications networking systems.

The thinking machine was an idea long before it became reality. We could go back as far as the nineteenth century, when Charles Babbage conceived of an Analytical Engine with many of the elements of contemporary digital computers. Babbage however was limited to Victorian technology and imagined an enormous machine worked by gears and levers. Not surprisingly, the concept was unrealized.[9] Alan Turing published a paper in 1937 postulating a machine that could carry out the discrete steps of mental computation as carried out by the human mind in a thinking operation. This imaginary machine has become known as the "universal Turing machine," a kind of Platonic mathematical form of the ideal digital computer of which all actual computers are imperfect approximations. During the war, working at the Bletchley Park code-breaking establishment, Turing was faced with the necessity of building an actual machine to keep up with the insatiable demands for quick decryption of German military communications. The result was the world's first digital computer, a huge machine employing 2,400 vacuum tubes, appropriately called COLOSSUS. Another military project begun at the University of Pennsylvania during the war and completed in 1946, in the earliest stages of the Cold War, created the ENIAC computer which dwarfed COLOSSUS: 18,000 vacuum tubes, 1,500 relays, 70,000 resistors, and 10,000 capacitators. Reportedly, lights across Philadelphia flickered when ENIAC was turned on. It could not store programs, and had to be programmed externally. The vacuum tubes burned out at an alarming rate. But the computer did complete the first task assigned it: computations for a mathematical model of a hydrogen bomb.

A half century later, there is more computational power, and certainly far greater reliability of performance in a single desktop PC than in the gymnasium-sized complex that was ENIAC. A number of key innovations have since transformed computing radically in terms of size and speed. The first was in 1947 at the Bell Laboratories in New Jersey, where the first transistor was developed as a cost-effective miniature replacement for the power-gobbling and unreliable vacuum tube. The first commercial use of the transistor was the cheap portable radio of the 1950s, an early sign of the coming age of ubiquitous and mobile media. A greater significance, not grasped immediately, was the capacity to construct smaller and cheaper computers.[10]

Through the 1960s, computing advanced, but remained at the large mainframe level. The 1970s appears as the real watershed with a number of key innovations concentrated in that decade. In the late 1960s, the first silicon-based microprocessor or microchip was developed, and marketed in 1971. A chip can hold many transistors, allowing the miniaturization of computing power. Chips can be embedded not only in computers but in virtually any object, thus giving rise to ubiquitous mini-computers from "smart cards" to "smart cars." Moore's Law, formulated in the 1960s, hypothesized that the number of transistors on a single chip would double every eighteen months. As explained in the *New York Times*:

> The transistor is the basic unit of information storage on a computer chip, one digit for each transistor. And so each 18-month interval brought a doubling of memory—with all the attendant increases in speed and efficiency that such a doubling entails. Today, Intel's most densely packed chips can contain 32 million transistors.
>
> Moore's Law also predicted that even as the power of computer chips would continue to grow significantly, their cost would fall at a spectacular rate—so much so that a single transistor, which sold for $70 in the mid-1960s, can now be bought for less than a millionth of a cent.
>
> Remarkable as it may seem, this law has held for 32 years, as the main frame begat the minicomputer, as the mini gave way to the PC and as chips have made their way into virtually all parts of modern electronic life.[11]

But Moore's Law is no longer valid. It has been rendered obsolete by new developments, such as "flash" technology that permits more than one digit to be stored on a single transistor; or "mega-chips" that operate at three times the speed of today's most powerful chips;[12] or quantum transistors that could be not only much faster than today's transistors but use much less power;[13] or research on even more microscopic transistor substitutes based on molecules[14] or, the latest and most remarkable of all, carbon "nanotubes" only a few atoms in diameter that could apparently be made to act as semiconductors.[15] Early in 1998, it was reported that "Israeli scientists have become the first to coax individual biological molecules into forming an electric circuit. This marriage of biotechnology and electronics will eventually make possible the production of a transistor sized 1/100,000th of the width of a human hair, 100th or less of the space required today."[16] Protein-based semiconductors may eventually replace silicon altogether with biomolecular computers.[17] There appears to be no end in sight for the upward trajectory of the miniaturization of computing power. If anything, the technology may already have surpassed the practical capacity to make short-term use of its full potential.

Another key innovation of the 1970s was the development of the microcomputer or PC in the mid-1970s and its marketing in the late 1970s, at the same time as operating systems became commercially available. By the late 1980s and early 1990s, ever more sophisticated software packages for everything from word processing to accounting to graphics design to games were widely available, and desktop PCs were being supplemented by highly mobile, light but powerful notebook computers that could travel anywhere. There was a shift from capital-intensive mainframe computing, with its close association with large hierarchical organizational bases (states, corporations, and large institutions) and authoritatively directed usage, to relatively cheap, widely diffused consumer technology that could be spontaneously directed to user-defined tasks: the democratization of computing.

The next step came from a unlikely marriage of the Cold War military research complex[18] and North American counterculture. The first linked computer network in 1969 was a research network under the aegis of the U.S. Department of Defense, called ARPANET. Horizontal networking proved irresistibly attractive to those who tasted its advantages, and by the early 1980s ARPANET, although still supported by the Defense Department, had become a scientific, rather than a military network, and had spawned other dedicated networks which all used ARPANET as their basic communications system. The emergent complex came to be called INTERNET. These developments were however still centered around large institutional nodes: government, military, and university research centers. Enter the counterculture. In the late 1970s, two university students invented the modem and then widely diffused at no charge the protocols that permit computers to transfer files directly without going through a host. Other students in 1979 created a protocol that allowed many computers to link together over the telephone. Spontaneous networks then grew together into a true network of all networks, the Internet, which quickly spread around the globe. What had begun within the shell of the Cold War military-research complex had burst these confines and become something absolutely unprecedented: a global communications nervous system of spontaneously generated networks constantly creating and recreating themselves.

At this point, the second critical stream of technological innovation comes into play: transmission capabilities. Digital information moves through various media mainly via cables or through the electromagnetic spectrum. Innovations in these areas have permitted vast increases in data transmitted ("bandwidth") and in the speed of transmission. Fiber optic cable can already transmit 1,000 times more bits per second than old-fashioned telephone cable—and counting, as no practical upwards limits have yet been glimpsed. Microwave transmissions and "bouncing" electromagnetic signals off satellites are the other important area for further exploitation and development.

Both these streams of technology have been developing in an exponential, explosive trajectory, but it is in the fusion of computing and communications ("networks"), that the truly revolutionary potential lies. Just as the capacity of the human mind to store, sort, retrieve, and manipulate vast amounts of information is being enormously enhanced by means of ever-smaller, ever-faster, and ever-more-powerful microprocessors, the reach of individuals is being immeasurably extended through fiber optic cable and satellite communication to form real-time networking of all computers.

This technological fusion has literally created a new world, a new space—*cyberspace*. Cyberspace exists nowhere and everywhere,[19] it is forever a tabula rasa in the sense that it is constantly being constructed and reconstructed, written and rewritten, by the simultaneous interaction of all those networking in the medium. The discovery of such a new world, and more, a world that is apparently plastic, is bound to bring out the Faustian in those who first glimpse its expansive, seemingly limitless contours.

> Then felt I like some watcher in the skies
> When a new planet swims into his ken[20]

With Faust, let us give the devil his due. The possibilities are endless, intoxicating. Space and distance—already shrunk by technologies such as the telephone—is finally dissolved in cyberspace. People communicate with one another without regard to physical location: communities (systems of communication?) can transcend not only locality but the artificial constructs of the nation and political boundaries; "virtual communities" consist of those drawn by common affinities wherever they happen to live. People can live parallel lives in which they invent on-line representations of themselves that interact with other on-line representations of other persons; they are reinventing themselves in another, parallel world that may, or may not, ever converge with the "real" world.[21] Virtual relationships may not be interactive with others, or even their online representations, at all. It is reported that a craze among girls in Japan is "boyfriend *tamagotchi*," or the virtual boyfriend, who only exists in cyberspace.[22] But it is not only human relationships that may be altered in profound but as yet unspecified ways. People interacting with computers and with one another through the medium of cyberspace develop altered notions of the self. New modes of expression are born out of the new forms of communication, and with them, changes to human consciousness.[23]

FROM ROBOTS TO CYBORGS

Already, not in some speculative future, but in the here and now, cyberspace is giving birth to new, "artificial" life forms. In computer labs, programs have been designed to replicate particular environments (say, an ocean) and into these environments a "species" (for instance, "fish") has been introduced that is programmed to adapt to changing conditions. Generations pass and adaptations are made quite independent of the original program. The fish swim about, eat, reproduce, and die in cyberspace. They are not "real", they have no physical materiality, yet they behave like "real" fish, they interact with their environment, and they make something of themselves in the process.[24] Instinctively, we tend to recoil from the idea of blurring the lines between "real life" and its "artificial" replication, but it is one of the extraordinary questions imposed by the new technologies and the new worlds they have opened up.

Another developing area is "intelligent software." Software programs personalized to an individual user's specifications are termed "software agents," in that they are designed to operate on behalf of the user in carrying out assignments. Software agents, sometimes called "knowbots" or simply "bots," act as digital proxies operating simultaneously in different places in cyberspace on behalf of their users. For example, a relatively simple software agent is a program that schedules meetings according to the unique habits of the user who may, for instance, prefer morning to afternoon scheduling. The agent automates the process, contacting prospective participants and arriving at mutually agreeable times. To carry out this task, the scheduling agent must be programmed with a capacity to learn and adapt to the peculiarities of the individuals involved. For instance, it must recognize that X is always unavailable for meetings on Tuesday mornings, or that Y has a strong preference for Fridays. Another kind of bot is designed to filter the heavy volume of information available on the Net according to the highly personalized interests of the user. For example, I might instruct a news-filtering bot to scan the daily newspapers on the net for stories about "terrorism." If it returns every story that happens to contain the word terror, I may wish to make its search more precise. An intelligent agent will be able to "learn" from its mistakes.

Bots are in effect trained to seek out certain kinds of information. For instance, someone might not have the time to do certain kinds of shopping on the Net for themselves: bots can be sent to fan out across the Web seeking the best bargains — and even doing the bargaining themselves. Or in the near future, stock brokers could be replaced by stockbots acting as virtual brokers.[25] What is especially interesting about bots is that they learn and adapt. As Pattie Maes, who is described as "Queen of the bots" for her work at the Software Agents Group at the MIT Media Lab, has written:

> Agent programs differ from regular software mainly by what can best be described as a sense of themselves as independent entities. An ideal agent knows what its goal is and will strive to achieve it. An agent should also be robust and adaptive, capable of learning from experience and respond-

ing to unforeseen situations with a repertoire of different methods. Finally, it should be autonomous so that it can sense the current state of its environment and act independently toward its goal.[26]

There is a Darwinian principle of evolution at work among bots, and a recent book has addressed the question of whether we are witnessing the origin of a "new species." Like robots, could bots go wrong? The case of the multiplying Barneys offers an amusing example. In one virtual online community, the program architects whimsically installed bots as the purple cartoon dinosaurs that went around singing, "I love you, you love me, we're a happy family." Other users grew so annoyed with the Barneys that they would virtually "punch" or "kick" them. "Whereupon the Barneys would break into parts, each of which would regenerate into a new Barney, until the community was overrun with Barneys."[27] This might seem comic, but not so funny is the unsettling notion of intelligent adaptive agents out there in cyberspace learning and evolving in autonomous ways. Moral and legal questions may be involved. What are the obligations of a user for actions taken by his or her "agent" in cyberspace transactions? Just another of the weird wonders of the new world.

These questions become even more troubling when we consider the collapsing boundaries between biology (the "natural") and the machine (the "artificial"). Coterminous with the Information Revolution is the Genetic Engineering Revolution and its offshoot, biotechnology. The public has become aware of some of the momentous and deeply unsettling consequences of biotechnology, particularly the possibility of human cloning, or of organ farming in which spare body parts are maintained for transplant. It is no accident that the two revolutions have been proceeding apace. Genetic research is based on decoding and reading DNA as the basic program, or software, for life. And computer technology is facilitating the mapping of the entire genetic structure. The Human Genome Project will not complete its work until some time in the twenty-first century — so far only about two percent of the herculean computing task has been accomplished. When it is completed, it will finally be possible to completely "read" DNA — and reading DNA means the ability to "write" DNA, which is to say, the power to design life according to specifications. Or, to shift language, the power to play God.

The 1980s film *Bladerunner*[28] depicts a Los Angeles of the twenty-first century where "replicants," genetically engineered people, are designed by the powerful Tyrell Corporation for profit. "More human than human is our motto," says the designer. The replicants are slaves, designed for particular tasks, but the most up-to-date models develop emotions and become rebellious; they are, however, designed with only four-year life spans. Rachel is an experimental replicant who thinks she is human; memory implants have manufactured a childhood and a past which she has taken to be her own. She learns of the deception, but she and a detective, Deckar (a "bladerunner" trained to hunt down and "retire" dangerous replicants) nevertheless fall in love. In a particularly haunting scene, after disclosing to Rachel that all her memories are implants out of which she has constructed an identity, Deckar remains alone with photographs of his own family and childhood. The viewer is left with the troubling suggestion that Deckar's past may be no more valid than Rachel's. Both have constructed identities out of fragmented elements of memory: are Deckar's faded photographs more "real" than Rachel's implants? Wherever she came from, Rachel is a self-conscious human, with a personality and an emotional chemistry that draws Deckar to the center of her melancholy, bewildered self. At the end of the film, Deckar flees a dark, decaying, acid-rain-drenched Los Angeles with Rachel. His fellow detective calls after them: "It's too bad she won't live. But then again, who does?"

The twin technologies of computing and genetics both point toward the creation of intelligence—artificial intelligence in the case of computing, and biologically engineered intelligence in the case of genetics. These are parallel paths but they are converging. In all likelihood, computer design will increasingly turn to the utilization of biological building blocks, such as protein-based microprocessors, for hardware and to analogies to the human brain (the world's most-advanced supercomputer, without a single silicon component) for developing artificial intelligence software, the next stage in computing power. Freeman Dyson speculates convincingly that while computer technology and genetics have been "engaged in a competition to take the leading role in the industrial revolution of the twenty-first century,"

> Neither genetics nor computers are likely to win the race outright. As the physical structures at the heart of modern computing become smaller, while the chemical structures at the heart of genetic engineering become more versatile, the two technologies are beginning to overlap and merge. It is likely that the winning designs for an intelligent solar-energy machine or an intelligent garbage-disposal machine will make use of electronic and biological tools working together. The self-reproducing machine will be partly made of genes and enzymes, while the genetically engineered brain and muscle will be partly made of integrated circuits and electric motors. In the end, physical and biological components will be so intimately entangled that we will be unable to say where one begins and the other ends.[29]

Already, scientists have been able to grow nerve cells of a rat on a silicon chip—and have transmitted electrical impulses through the cells to the chip. Eventually, it should be possible to take human brain cells and connect them directly to a computer. Silicon chips, for instance, could be implanted in the brain, thus combining different kinds of intelligence. Silicon is better at data storage and retrieval, as well as at calculation, while the brain is more adept at pattern recognition. Why not see if they could be made to work together, thus producing a "bionic" brain, one that could combine the best of quantitative and qualitative intelligence?[30]

From the late 1940s until sometime in the 1960s, the Western imagination conceived of computers first as calculating machines, then as robots, machines that could both think and act. Robots need not just sit passively awaiting human instruction. Like humans, they could move about, acting positively on the world. Unlike the human mind, robot intelligence could be applied uncomplainingly to routine, repetitive, or dangerous tasks. Practical applications of robot technology were everywhere. Might not factory robots work assembly lines with greater efficiency than human workers, and require less care in their handling? Assembly-line robots would not become tired or bored and make mistakes, as their human counterparts were all to prone to do. Tiresome household chores might be taken over

by robot butlers and cooks. Tasks that were unpleasant or dangerous for biological creatures to perform — mining certain materials,
for instance, or toxic cleanups and bomb disposals — might be more
safely and efficiently accomplished by robots.

Robots were alternately welcomed and feared. Welcomed because they promised to eliminate drudgery and facilitate work and
life. Feared because they could be seen as replacing human workers
altogether, taking over and ruling the world. A joke that circulated
among computer scientists in the early mainframe days went like
this: at some point in the far distant future, all the computers in the
galaxy are connected together in a series. When the switch is thrown
to activate the ultimate supercomputer, the first question fed into it
is the age-old question that always obsessed humanity: "Is there a
God?" The sky darkens, thunder rumbles, and the answer comes
back: "NOW there is!" Science fiction in the 1950s was replete with
lurid tales of robots triumphing over humanity. The robots were
usually depicted as human analogs, but caricatures: they were more
often than not metal men, with arms, legs, and heads, but at once
smarter and more powerful than people yet emotionless, without
any of the sparks of passion, love, or hatred that burned within real
people. It was as if robots were a chilling embodiment of humanity's
Promethean capacities to conjure up the powers of science and
mathematical rationality which then broke their bonds and returned as threat. It was surely no accident that the imagined menace
of the robot coincided historically with the atomic age. When J.
Robert Oppenheimer, the "father of the Bomb" witnessed the
huge, sinister mushroom cloud rising over the first atomic test at
Alamogordo in 1945, a line from the Hindu *Bhagavad Gita* flashed
in his mind:

I am become Death, the shatterer of worlds[31]

Robots were feared as the messengers of death as well: death from
science and reason run amuck; death as the triumph of metal over
flesh; death as the victory of the cold and inert over the warm and
the vital.

The ultimate depiction of the robot as death-dealer was in the
1960s film *2001: A Space Odyssey*, where the famous HAL, the voice-

synthesized computer tending the spaceship heading toward Jupiter, decides that the crew is getting in his way and starts methodically killing them.[32] HAL is also a representational watershed because he is depicted as an omnipresent, panoptic eye, ear, and mind that are essential to the functioning of the ship and its human inhabitants. HAL's embedded presence points toward a more contemporary understanding of artificial intelligence. As the information revolution continues into the twenty-first century, it will be more and more difficult to conceive of man versus machine in the old way. The "computer" as a discrete entity—CPU, screen, keyboard, and other accessories—that sits on one's desk, or fits in a carrying case, is doomed to go the way of all obsolescent technologies. The future will be "ubiquitous computing," intelligence embedded throughout our working and living environments.[33] Smart cards, such as credit cards with information embedded on a chip, or identity cards containing personal information, are just the start. Smart cars, smart offices, schools and factories, and smart houses will offer environments in which there are no stand-alone computers, but computing power that is everywhere. We are even moving into an era of smart building materials, for example: bridges that can sense changes in wind velocity and adjust structural tension automatically, or smart paint that exudes a fire retardant when it senses too much heat.[34] This future too is one that can inspire dread. In Philip Kerr's 1995 sci-fi thriller *The Grid*,[35] a smart building in Los Angeles is monitored and run by an artificial intelligence that, like HAL, becomes a malevolent killer. But this may be an atavistic reaction, an anthropomorphism that substitutes for a failure of the imagination when confronting a new reality that has no precedent in past experience.

As the old image of the robot has receded, it is being replaced by a construct that is located at the intersection of developing technology and imagination: the cyborg. The cyborg is part human, part machine, perhaps even part animal. The concept of the cyborg rests on an understanding that, in Donna Haraway's words:

> there is no fundamental, ontological separation in our formal knowledge
> of machine and organism, of technical and organic. . . . One conse-

quence is that our sense of connection to our tools is heightened. . . . Why should our bodies end at the skin, or include at best other beings encapsulated by skin? From the seventeenth century till now, machines could be animated—given ghostly souls to make them speak or move or to account for their orderly development and mental capacities. Or organisms could be mechanized—reduced to body understood as resource of the mind. These machine/organism relationships are obsolete, unnecessary. For us, in imagination and in other practice, machines can be prosthetic devices, intimate components, friendly selves.[36]

Already the cyborg appears as a cultural stereotype. The movie and the TV series *RoboCop* depict a mechanical, robot-like figure with superhuman power. But buried inside RoboCop is a human who has been reconstituted by mechanical extensions to become larger, faster, and more lethal than life. He also becomes something less than fully human, as his original identity is lost and then only partially recovered within his new mechanical carapace. More complex than this somewhat simplistic vehicle for male violence fantasies are the variations played out in the films *Terminator 1* and *Terminator 2*. Here cyborgs of the future come back to 1980s and 1990s Los Angeles to rewrite the past in order to assure the victory of artificial over human intelligence. The original Terminator (Arnold Schwarzenegger) is a robot-like creature programmed to kill. In *Terminator 2*, he is reprogrammed to become the "good guy" but must now confront an even more lethal and advanced cyborg from the future that embodies the fusion of the machine with the biological: this Terminator "morphs" effortlessly from one form to another, mimicking precisely existing forms, whether of people or objects.

The cyborg has most often been appropriated in popular culture as a more up-to-date version of the robot, set apart from and against "normal" or "natural" humans. But while old stereotypes die hard, there are other ways in which the cyborg as form is being assimilated more intimately into the fabric of how we understand ourselves. Feminist writer Donna Haraway in the 1980s developed the cyborg as a kind of blasphemous antiracist feminist figure.[37] The cyborg as symbol of disappearing boundaries, as a form that challenges "nature" as something fixed, also challenges fixed notions of gender and race. The cyborg is suggestive of multiculturalism in a profound sense (although it may well be appropriated by capitalism to sell multiculturalism in a superficial sense).

Another way to understand the cyborg is ecological: we are not autonomous identities clearly bounded by an inside and an outside; we are instead parts of a larger social ecosystem that combines nature, humanity, and the "artificial" extensions of humanity together in a cybernetic relational web. Cyberspace is the plane on which these aspects intersect most visibly. Nowhere is this more memorably depicted than in a short story by William Gibson, "The Winter Market."[38] Lise is/was a woman but when Gibson's hero Casey first sees her, she is already a cyborg woman, her sick, drug-addled body encased in a polycarbon exoskeleton that enables her to move and act (barely) in the world. She picks up Casey at a party and returns with him to his place. He refuses her offer of sex, but a relationship far more intimate awaits them. Casey is an editor of people's dreams, which he reconstructs in virtual reality technology to be sold as commodities by a giant multimedia corporation. Dream artists have become global pop stars. Lise turns out to be a mega dream-artist star with a mammoth hit called *Kings of Sleep*, and as her editor, Casey falls into a strange attraction/repulsion relationship with her. Like her audience, he is in love with her dreams, but the relationship with the "real" Lise remains distant, awkward, and sexless. She is destroying her already decaying body with massive drug abuse, almost as if she hated what remained of her biological self. Then Casey learns from the corporation that "she'd merged with the net, crossed over for good." Lise, body finally abandoned, is downloaded into cyberspace. But she is neither dead nor alive in the conventional sense. Casey is warned that he will receive a call from her in the near future,

> when you have to edit her next release. Which will almost certainly be soon because she needs money bad. She's taking up a lot of ROM on some corporate mainframe, and her share of *Kings* won't come close to paying for what they had to do to put her there.

Casey, stunned, asks: "if she calls me, is it *her*?" The response: "God only knows. I mean, Casey, the technology is there, so who, man, really who, is to say?"

This is a moral parable indeed for the age of cyberspace. Immortality can be purchased but only by an ultimate act of commodification.

THE DISMAL SCIENCE
IN THE LIBRARY OF BABEL

Borges' Library of Babel presents itself as the universe itself. But of course it is not really the "universe"—its architecture is not the architecture of matter. It is an analogical "universe." Its shelves store information in the form of texts which contain "data" that mirror or reproduce the material universe. Borges' nature of the Library exists *ab aeterno*. The architecture of information is too complex and elegant to have been the product of man, the "imperfect librarian." Call it God or Nature as you please, but remember that information is about something, it is not that thing itself. But this is easily obscured when the focus shifts to what is in the Library. Borges also states that "The orthographical symbols are twenty-five in number" (the letters of the alphabet plus the period, comma, and space). This has allowed the formulation of a General Theory of the Library. That is, all books are made up of the same elements, but in the "vast Library there are no two identical books." From these premises it may be deduced that the "Library is total and that its shelves register all the possible combinations of the twenty-odd orthographical symbols. . . ." In other words, "all that it is given to express, in all languages. Everything: the minutely detailed history of the future. . . ."

> When it was proclaimed that the Library contained all books, the first impression was one of extravagant happiness. All men felt themselves to be the masters of an intact and secret treasure. There was no personal or world problem whose elegant solution did not exist in some hexagon. The universe was justified, the universe suddenly usurped the unlimited dimension of hope.

Thus our own era of infohype, the unlimited promise of the great Internet (the embodiment of Borges' Library condensed into millions of individual computer screens as [W]indows into cyberspace, a "sphere whose exact centre is any one of its hexagons and whose circumference is inaccessible"). These are no small matters. The devil's promises are enthralling. No wonder so many have been drawn by the siren's song. But wait . . . cyberspace is not another universe into which we can escape via a magic doorway. Dream worlds exist in the minds of dreamers, who live in *this* world, breathe, eat when hungry, and drink when thirsty — or not, depending on their material circumstances. Cyberspace is a dreamed world, but the dreamers dream it through the mediation of computer hardware, fiber optic cable, complex telecommunications networks, and specific social and economic systems that support and deliver these technologies. Cybernauts are *wired*, in more ways than one. There is, or at least there should be, a *political economy* of cyberspace. Yes, even in the free-floating delirium of this new world, the old dismal science, like gravity, drags the cybernauts back toward earth.

Some uncomfortable but unavoidable facts: most of the people of the present real world not only lack computers but even lack access to telephones. To most of the world, the Information Revolution is not even a rumor. The so-called Information Superhighway that U.S. Vice President Al Gore pumps like carnival barker may be opening out like a vast autobahn for the wealthier classes in North America, Europe, and the hyper-developed parts of Asia, but when it reaches into Africa, Latin America, and the less-developed parts of Asia, it reaches as narrow fingers into privileged islands; for much of the Third World, it simply stops short altogether.[39] Nor is there any rational reason to think that the Information Revolution offers a magical solution to the endemic problems of poverty and underdevelopment. It is rather the latest name given to the enduring and ever-deepening domination of the many poor by the wealthy few. Access to the Internet is as much use to a Bangladeshi peasant as hitching a ride on the Challenger space shuttle; but it is very useful to the multinational corporations that rule the global economic system that maintains Bangladesh as a ghetto of misery.

This is clearly true even within Western societies. A reasonably up-to-date computer clone, pirated software, modem, and monthly connect charge may not represent a huge investment. Yet it excludes a great many, as does the specific context of computer culture. The result is that the Internet has a decidedly middle-class look. Further, users tend to be disproportionately male, white, and the other familiar categories of privilege. Of course, over time these things may change. But just as with the case for Third World development, there are overheated notions afloat in political and bureaucratic circles (viz., the frenetic mind of Newt Gingrich) that a computer in every kitchen will somehow solve the problem of unemployment and regional economic decline. It is, of course, out of the question that right-wing neoliberal politicians, some of whom babble about the transformative power of the computer, can devise and execute and pay for a vast public-works scheme for actually putting the hardware and software required into the hands of the poor and the unemployed. Unfortunately, social democrats have been equally complicit, if less utopian, in talking up the computer as empowerment. Even the limited schemes undertaken by some social democratic governments to "retrain" (a mantra of contemporary capitalist crisis) redundant fishermen with no fish stocks, coal miners with closed pits, or workers with skills tied to vanishing heavy industries, by imparting "computer skills" quickly exhibit their limitations. At best, these retrained workers hunching over their consoles have instantaneous access to the intelligence that no jobs are available. At least lining up outside the unemployment office provided some minimal human contact with others of like predicament, even if the end result is the same.

The attraction of neoliberal politicians to infobabble has little to do with any notions of redistribution of wealth and power. The computer as "empowerment" is a wonderfully ambiguous piece of rhetoric. This "empowerment" offers a convenient and trendy rationale for further slashing the public sector. Who needs armies of public sector workers to offer support services when former state clients have the opportunity to plug in directly? Who needs expensive capital investment in physical infrastructure and maintenance when services can be accessed on the Net? Right-wing politicians in North America who are tired of seeing tax dollars going to universities and colleges have started talking about the "Virtual University," where courses are on offer to clients (formerly called students) receiving information designed by programmers (formerly called professors), tapping in assignments, and answering exam questions without ever leaving their home computers. In the fullness of this vision, the entire support and maintenance staffs, most of the teaching staff, and the administrative apparatus can be lopped off the public rolls, and the physical plant (formerly known as the campus) can be sold to the private sector for more productive and profitable use. This is a paradigm for other such schemes for a "Virtual Public Sector" or the "Virtual State." Like virtual reality, users allow their senses to delude them into believing that they are somewhere they are not, that they are really doing things that are not happening at all. The opiate of the masses, indeed.

There is an ideology among many of today's cybernauts, especially the Americans, that can best be described as frontier capitalism, or rugged individualism. The self image is that of the lone frontiersman out there on the cutting edge of civilization armed with his contemporary equivalent of the six-gun, the high-speed modem. It is expressed in a powerful aversion to the traditional enemy of the frontiersman, government and its attempts to regulate and domesticate his wild energies. Thus there have been ferocious reactions to the clumsy attempts of the Clinton administration to impose surveillance over the Internet from the "clipper chip" and the embargoeing of exports of various encryption programs; to the FBI's hamhanded attempt to enforce tapping of digital communication (and make the users pay for the privilege!); to censorship initiatives from various levels of government against cyberspace pornography and hate mail.[40] These are probably reasonable responses under the circumstances, but they are also classic examples of navigating via the rearview mirror.

Neither individual free enterprise nor an aggressive interventionist state are particularly relevant to the new political economy of cyberspace. Hardware and software are produced by corporate giants such as IBM and Microsoft, and the infrastructure of the Internet is currently a bone of contention between the telephone and media/cable giants. The real frontier is the commodification of information by capital. To shift metaphors, cyberspace is like the commons under attack from enclosures. The relentless emphasis in recent years on "intellectual property" as a crucial element in international trade agreements points us clearly in the direction that the so-called Information Revolution is travelling. The architecture of cyberspace may well look very much like William Gibson's fictional vision: vast, mysterious collections of data looming like mega-fortresses fiercely guarded by giant corporations—while the "real world" wallows in urban squalor, petty criminality, violence, and tawdry escapism.

FROM MASS TO MICRO

Information is a resource whose relation to late twentieth-century capitalism is like that of oil to the capitalism of the early twentieth century. This is not to say, as some have unwisely extrapolated, that industrial capitalism is dead. Automobiles still provide the basic means of transportation for much of the world, and oil must still be tapped to feed the voracious appetite of automobiles for fuel. Information has not displaced older resources, just as postindustrialism has not displaced industrialism. But the computer and the new communications technologies have redefined how production and distribution take place. Mass production and mass consumption have, in the process of fulfilling their promise of growth, been transmuted. Production (including services) requires fewer workers and greater "flexibility," and mass consumption of mass-marketed goods is increasingly matched by "niche" marketing of specifically targeted production. On both sides of the equation, information and high-speed communication of that information are crucial resources. The shift from primary production to the information-intensive services sector that is evident throughout the rich industrial nations is another indicator of this same change. Command over information and its transmission will be the key to success in the capitalist world of tomorrow.

The notion that this crucial resource will be allowed to become a public good is idealism at its most inane.[42] Thus the cyberspace commons is enclosed as rapidly as its space expands. The advocates of "electronic freedom" have their hearts in the right place but their heads in the sand. More apposite to the realities are the young freelance cyberpunk hackers who for their own fun and profit break into the dark corporate information towers that loom over the wired world. During the threatened U.S. attack on Iraq in early 1998, a concerted cyber assault on Pentagon data bases led to initial alarms about "infowar" by America's enemies. It turned out to be two teen-age hackers. When one, calling himself Makaveli, was questioned about political motives, he scornfully replied: "It's power dude, you know, power"[43]—by which he presumably meant power for its own sake, not for any larger motive. Makaveli's mentor, a young Israeli calling himself The Analyzer, was praised by Israeli Prime Minister Benjamin Netanyahu, and judged by many in his country to be a folk hero. In one interview, The Analyzer declared that he "hated" big organizations and governments and suggested "chaos" as a good alternative to government.[44] Yet even these latter-day in-formation highwaymen are sometimes themselves gobbled up by the very organizations they have successfully targeted: the elec-tronic safe-crackers are hired on as smart high-tech security guards to keep out others (and, who knows, to crack their competitor's se-curity as well?). Already we may be moving into a new era that leaves behind the individualistic hacking frontier: organized elec-tronic warfare employing disciplined teams of corporate hackers setting about systematically to break into or to sabotage the data banks and operational software of economic competitors may be-come the order of the day.[45] The world of financial data companies was rocked in 1998 by news that a U.S. federal undercover investi-gation, including confidential informants and taped conversations, had revealed that one financial data giant, a subsidiary of Reuters, had allegedly commissioned computer specialists to steal confiden-tial information from the corporate computers of a major competi-tor, Bloomberg.[46] What was shocking were public allegations against a respectable financial services firm, although this kind of corporate cyber-espionage may well be more frequent than is gen-erally admitted. Computer viruses, first transmitted by freelancers out of malice or just for the hell of it, may increasingly be utilized as weapons targeted at specific competitive information systems (the biological warfare of cyberspace, attacking the synapses of the en-emy's information economy).[47] There is a growing literature on "infowar" as a new frontier in international hostility, and even a guru of the new military science, Winn Schwartau.[48] Techniques that target and disrupt enemy information systems need not be limited to states. They are adaptable to corporate competition as well. The threat of infowar tactics has already encouraged a growing attention to protective security measures, such as the construction of firewalls around data. State-sector communications intelligence agencies are now offering their considerable expertise in information security to the private sector on a cost-recovery basis. The information security section of Britain's Government Communications Headquarters (GCHQ) is now financially self-supporting on the basis of charges for its advice to British companies.[49] These developments are not surprising, given the opportunities for aggression opened up by the new technologies. But it is a long way from the "promise of the Internet," from the limitless vistas of information laid open to each and all who wish to browse its fields and pluck its free flowers of truth.

We should consider carefully why the promise of the Internet is such a pleasing delusion. It is not because capitalists are evil people, or because corporations are conspiring against the public interest (both propositions might be true, but still are beside the point). Information is a product. Raw, unprocessed data is not yet information—and even that requires someone to collect it in the first instance and store it in accessible form. Already there are claimants expecting compensation for their work. Processing data into a finished product useful to potential consumers is even greater value added. All this will be reflected in the final price. Only in the for-profit private sector are there the resources both to produce sophisticated information and to purchase the finished product on a commercially viable scale. Public-sector information services were once fairly widely available on a free or relatively low-cost basis, but in this neoliberal era, market principles of user-pay, cost recovery, and servicing "clients" have led to the virtual privatization of public-sector information. Even those once-privileged bastions of state information secrecy, the security and intelligence agencies, are flogging their information services to the highest bidders in the private sector.[50] Governments increasingly post free information on the Internet, but this is mainly for democratic legitimation of their cost-recovery supply to the private sector: the very fact that information is freely available is generally proof of its relatively low value as commodity.

Cyberspace will be a treasure trove of information for those who already have treasuries to spend. For the rest of us, the promise of the Internet may too often mean an overstuffed, cluttered, anarchically disorganized jumble of infotrash, so worthless that it has been discarded to lie along the sidewalks of the information highway for the casual use of anyone who cares to pick up the odd item. As time goes by, some of this litter will be cleaned up and replaced by smaller business ventures selling baubles and beads: North American television viewers have already seen the future in the shopping channels. Even the *Inter*net as we now know it may be increasingly displaced by private *Intra*nets. Intranets are extensions of local networks that use the same Web technology as Internet users, but are limited to authorized internal use. Transnational corporations like Xerox can offer all the communications services of the Web to employees wherever they are located, and even extend these to suppliers and clients on a limited basis, within secure boundaries. In the late 1990s, Intranets have become so popular that installations of servers limited to internal use have outpaced external Web servers. This points to a future architecture of the Web in which the information "commons" is increasingly hedged by enclosures into which ordinary commoners cannot gain entry except by membership or by paying for the privilege.

THE NET AS METAPHOR

It is perhaps a mistake to become too fixated on the "Net" as the 1990s Internet, or the Web as the 1990s World Wide Web. The latter are particular embodiments of the possibilities of the new information technologies, at a particular technological moment. They will most certainly change, perhaps unrecognizably, and sooner rather than later in the febrile, Darwinian world of high-technology innovation. Much more interesting is the network as a metaphor for a new form of organization that is being enabled by the new information technologies. I say "enabled" advisedly: network organization has been with us for some time, but the new technologies have enabled its growing dominance and its displacement of older forms of organization.

Manuel Castells titled the first volume of his monumental three-volume study of the Information Age *The Rise of the Network Society*. To Castells, a new information technology paradigm has taken shape with pervasive effects, including

> the *networking logic* of any system or set of relationships using these new information technologies. The morphology of the network seems to be well adapted to increasing complexity of interaction and to unpredictable patterns of development arising from the creative power of such interaction. This topological configuration, the network, can now be materially implemented, in all kinds of processes and organizations, by newly available information technologies. Without them, the networking logic would be too cumbersome to implement. Yet this networking logic is needed to structure the unstructured while preserving flexibility, since the unstructured is the driving force of innovation in human activity.[51]

Castells works out the ramifications of the logic of networking on a global scale, even to the point where it begins to reconfigure our conception of space, which he argues has moved from a "space of places" to a "*space of flows*": "the spatial articulation of dominant functions does take place in our societies in the network of interactions made possible by information technology devices. In this network, no place exists by itself, since the positions are defined by flows."[52]

Older forms of organization, big states and big corporations in particular, are sorely pressed by the networking logic either to recreate themselves or to break. Corporations have adapted much better and more quickly than states and public bodies. In part this is due to their greater sensitivity to market pricing. Markets themselves are network-like structures that train their users to think in terms of flows of supply and demand. The first great casualty of the information age were the sclerotic command economies of the Soviet bloc. These bureaucratic dinosaurs, which had once preserved themselves through isolation from global markets (both self-imposed and in part externally imposed during the earlier phases of the Cold War) simply could not cope with the strains imposed on them. Western governments have begun to change and adapt, although not perhaps at the rate that the corporate sector has.

Among the key elements in network organization is a declining emphasis on vertical hierarchical authority structures and a rising emphasis on *horizontal linkages that cut across traditional organizational boundaries.* The older organizational form emphasized command and control from the top and strictly defined organizational boundaries. The military and police remain the most extreme examples of a disciplined, hierarchical organizational structure with a strong sense of an exclusive organizational identity (often called esprit de corps). The traditional corporation was less militant, but very conscious of its organizational integrity. Vertical integration of operations ensured overall control over all aspects of production, distribution, and marketing. Newer organizational forms undermine both hierarchy and boundaries in two ways. First, within the organization, horizontal communication is facilitated by the new technologies and there is more scope for cooperative work groups, moderating traditional hierarchical authority. Second, services formerly done in-house are increasingly drawn from outside, which blurs the organizational boundaries. By contrast to the older form, the networked organization is decentered both internally and externally. These changes are illustrated by a recent report about Montsanto, a cutting-edge biotechnology corporation. Explaining Monsanto's corporate strategy, one executive indicated that "building a network of companies we can work with around the world is a key job for us." Another executive speculated that the company "may even one day experiment with having employees choose their own managers and with shaping budgets by how many people want to work on a project."[53] In management terms, the "new enterprise is a network of distributed teams that act as clients and servers for each other."[54]

In the networked economy, molecularly structured work groups are formed and reformed to meet (and anticipate) particular challenges. Partnerships and strategic alliances are formed for particular projects, creating "virtual corporations." "Disintermediation" is a (somewhat barbarous) word coined to describe the obsolescence of middlemen now short- circuited by direct networking communication. Dell Computers has built a multibillion-dollar global business selling hardware to order directly through the telephone and the Internet. Corporations that once existed to produce particular products (this company manufactured cars, that company telephones) now find their organizational form following the dictates of product innovation, rather than the reverse. Thus what were once electronic hardware companies, software developers, telephone and TV cable carriers, and entertainment corporations, now all converge to offer integrated services.

All these features imply *flexibility*, a term that has taken on a certain notoriety as implying, and rationalizing, unemployment and large-scale disruptions of settled patterns of life. A flexible labor force is seen as an expendable labor force. The era of innovation in information technologies has coincided with the ascendancy of the neoliberal agenda of corporate and state restructuring as downsizing. The new technologies have often been employed as justification for layoffs and closures. Whether this is reason or rationale is another matter. The question of whether the new technologies are the determining factor in the creation of permanent unemployment and persistent downward pressure on living standards of workers, or whether the latter are more the result of particular policy frameworks adopted by powerful elites, is a large and complex issue that cannot be dealt with here. But one thing is clear: the logic of networking does strongly demand flexibility, in management and in the workforce, not to speak of schools and all other institutions of the network society. Flexibility demands constant adjustment to change, and this in turn implies a state of permanent insecurity, an insecurity that is endemic, pervasive, and inescapable.

Here we confront a central paradox in the network society. Although the form demands and rewards flexibility and innovation, the insecurity engendered by its effects promotes a very different kind of behavior: risk-aversion. The volatility and unpredictability inherent in networks create an urgent organizational imperative to seek at least tolerable degrees of stability and predictability. The paradox is acute. The new information technologies that promote change and risk at one level also provide the technical means to reduce risk factors at another level. Information-driven systems are self-monitoring and self-correcting, which is what makes them so adaptable, but continual monitoring also gives them the capacity to identify, isolate, and eliminate risk factors within the organizational structure and increased capacity to scan the external environment to avoid potential risk factors. The new information technologies are also technologies of surveillance, which I discuss in detail in the next chapter.

NOTES TO CHAPTER 3

1. Parts of this chapter are drawn from Reg Whitaker, "The Tower of InfoBabel: Cyberspace as Alternative Universe," in Leo Panitch, ed., *Socialist Register 1996: Are There Alternatives?* (London: Merlin Press, 1996), 173–88.

2. See for instance Nicholas Negroponte, *Being Digital* (N.Y.: Vintage Books, 1995). A slightly more balanced and cautious vision is offered by the Canadian management consultant, Don Tapscott *The Digital Economy: Promise and Peril in the Age of Networked Intelligence* (N.Y.: McGraw-Hill, 1996).

3. It is admittedly hard to find a single representative source for this perspective. Perhaps the closest would be Howard Rheingold, *The Virtual Community: Homesteading on the Electronic Frontier* (Reading, Mass.: Addison-Wesley, 1993). Rheingold's politics are a kind of American anarchism; it is notable that there are few "old left" or Marxist enthusiasts for the Net.

4. David F. Noble, *Progress Without People: New Technology, Unemployment, and the Message of Resistance* (Toronto: Between the Lines, 1995). Noble proudly accepts the title of "Luddite," from the early nineteenth-century machine-smashers.

5. Clifford Stoll, *Silicon Snake Oil: Second Thoughts on the Information Highway* (N.Y.: Doubleday, 1995). Stoll was himself author of a kind of true-life technological thriller, *The Cuckoo's Egg: Tracking a Spy Through the Maze of Computer Espionage* (N.Y.: Doubleday, 1989).

6. Jorge Luis Borges, *Labyrinths: Selected Stories and Other Writings* (N.Y.: New Directions, 1964), 51–58.

7. This is true only "in a sense," in that the digital code itself must be stored.

8. For a thoughtful description of the meanings of digitization see Jim Davis and Michael Stack, "The Digital Advantage," in Jim Davis, Thomas A. Hirschl and Michael Stack, *Cutting Edge: Technology, Information Capitalism and Social Revolution* (London: Verso, 1997), 121–44.

9. Cyberpunk novelists William Gibson & Bruce Sterling, *The Difference Engine* (N.Y.: Bantam Books, 1991) imagine a counterfactual Victorian England in which Babbage's machine was not only built but widely diffused.

10. Lee Dye, "50 Years Ago, Information Age Began in Bell Labs," *Los Angeles Times*, 22 December 1997. Michael Riordan and Lillian Hoddeson, *Crystal Fire: The Birth of the Information Age* (N.Y.: W. W. Norton & Company, 1997).

11. John Markoff, "New Chip May Make Today's Computer Passe," *New York Times*, 17 September 1997.

12. John Markoff, "IBM and Digital to Report on New Super-Chips," *New York Times*, 4 February 1998.

13. Mark Prigg, "A New Device Based on Quantum Physics Promises a Revolution in Processing Speed," *The Sunday Times*, 22 February 1998; John Markoff, "Quantum Computers Leap From Theory to a Powerful Potential," *New York Times*, 28 April 1998.

14. John Markoff, "Tiny Magnets May Bring Computing Breakthrough," *New York Times*, 27 January 1997.

15. Malcolm W. Browne, "Next Electronics Breakthrough: Power-Packed Carbon Atoms," *New York Times*, 17 February 1998.

16. Judy Siegel, "Technion Scientists 'Coax' Molecules to Form Electric Circuit," *Jerusalem Post*, 19 February 1998.

17. Robert R. Birge, "Protein-based computers," *Scientific American* (March 1995) 90–95.

18. For an excellent analysis of how computers developed within the terms of Cold War discourse and in turn shaped that discourse, see Paul N. Edwards, *The Closed World: Computers and the Politics of Discourse in Cold War America* (Cambridge, Mass.: The MIT Press, 1996).

19. See Julian Stallabrass, "Empowering Technology: The Exploration of Cyberspace," *New Left Review* 211 (May/June 1995) 3–32.

20. Keats, "On First Looking into Chapman's Homer", H. W. Carrod, ed., *The Poetical Works of John Keats* (Oxford: Claundon Press, 1939) p. 45.

21. In Douglas Coupland's novel *Microserfs* (N.Y.: Harper Collins, 1995), set among a group of ex-Microsoft "techies" running their own software start-up in Silicon Valley, one character falls in love with an e-mail correspondent in Waterloo, Ontario, whom he knows only by the address BARCODE, sex, age, etc. unspecified. In the novel, the pair meet and everything works out. So it has sometimes been in real life, although cyber relationships often prudently remain just that.

22. Glenda Cooper, "Cyberpets Superseded as Girls Seek Perfect Boy for Virtual Romance," *The Independent,* 19 December 1997.

23. Mark Poster, *The Mode of Information: Poststructuralism and Social Context* (Chicago University of Chicago Press, 1990); Sherry Turkle, *Life on the Screen: Identity in the Age of the Internet* (N.Y.: Simon & Schuster, 1995) and her earlier *The Second Self: Computers and the Human Spirit* (N.Y.: Simon & Schuster, 1984).

24. Claus Emmeche, *The Garden in the Machine: The Emerging Science of Artificial Life* (Princeton, N.J.: Princeton University Press 1994). The virtual fish actually do exist, in a computer at the University of Toronto: see Stephen Strauss, "Artificial Life," *The Globe and Mail* (Toronto) 10 September 1994. Demetri Terzopoulos, Xiayuan Tu, and Ralph Grzeszczuk, "Artificial Fishes with Autonomous Locomotion, Perception, Behavior, and Learning in a Simulated Physical World," in Rodney A. Brooks and Patti Maes, eds., *Artificial Life: Proceedings of the 4th International Workshop on the Synthesis and Simulation of Living Systems* (Cambridge, Mass.: The MIT Press, 1994), 17–27.

25. Carol Alvarez Troy, "Envisioning Stock Trading Where the Brokers Are Bots," *New York Times,* 16 November 1997.

26. Pattie Maes, "Intelligent Software," *Scientific American* (September 1995), 85. See

also Maes, "Agents That Reduce Work and Information Overload," in Jeffrey M. Bradshaw, ed., *Software Agents* (Menlo Park, Calif.: AAAI Press/The MIT Press, 1997), 145–64.

27. Christopher Lehmann-Haupt, "Cyberspace Through a Darwinian Lens," *New York Times*, 19 September 1997, reviewing Andrew Leonard, *Bots: The Origin of New Species*.

28. Directed by Ridley Scott, *Bladerunner* was based on a science fiction novel by Philip K. Dick, *Do Androids Dream of Electric Sheep?* This was perhaps one case where a film surpassed the book on which it was based, certainly in terms of its eerie resonances that continue to reverberate long after the film's initial appearance. Not surprisingly, *Bladerunner* continues as a cult object on a number of Internet websites.

29. Freeman Dyson, *Imagined Worlds* (Cambridge, Mass.: Harvard University Press, 1997), 120–21.

30. Steve Connor, "Brain Chip Signals Arrival of Bionic Man," *Sunday Times*, 16 November 1997; Sandeep Junnarkar, " 'GeneChip Encodes DNA on Silicon," *New York Times*, 15 March 1997; Sandra Blakeslee, "Bionic Chip Built to Aid Brain Study," *New York Times*, 2 December 1997.

31. Robert Jungk, *Brighter Than a Thousand Suns: A Personal History of the Atomic Scientists* (Harmondsworth, Middlesex: Penguin, 1960), 183.

32. David G. Stork, ed., *HAL's Legacy: 2001's Computer as Dream and Reality* (Cambridge, Mass.: MIT Press, 1998).

33. Vinton G. Cerf, "When They're Everywhere," in Peter J. Denning and Robert M. Metcalfe, eds., *Beyond Calculation: The Next Fifty Years of Computing* (N.Y.: Springer-Verlag, 1997), 33–42.

34. John Markoff, "New Wave in High-Tech: Deus Ex (Tiny) Machina," *New York Times*, 27 January 1997.

35. (N.Y.: Bantam Books, 1997); originally in the U.K. in 1995 as *Gridiron*.

36. Donna J. Haraway, "A Cyborg Manifesto: Science, Technology, and Socialist-Feminism in the Late Twentieth Century," in Haraway, *Simians, Cyborgs, and Women: the Reinvention of Nature* (N.Y.: Routledge, 1990), 178. See also Scott McCracken, "Cyborg Fictions: The Cultural Logic of Posthumanism," in Leo Panitch, ed., *Socialist Register 1997: Ruthless Criticism of All That Exists* (London: Merlin Press, 1997), 288–301.

37. Haraway, "Cyborg Manifesto."

38. "The winter market," in William Gibson, *Burning Chrome* (N.Y.: Ace Books, 1987).

39. A recent survey indicated there are about 3.4 million computers hooked up to the Internet in the United States (seventy percent of the global total) and just over 500,000 in Western Europe. By contrast, Africa has just 27,100, Central and South America 16,000, and the Middle East 13,800. A report by a nongovernmental foundation warned about a new form of poverty — "information poverty" — that threatens the developing world. "There is a danger of a new information elitism which excludes the majority of the world's population. . . . The technology could actually increase the gap between rich and poor." Mark John, "Third World Faces Information Poverty — report," Reuters (London) 11 October 1995. Even this survey may have missed the degree of domination of the Internet by U.S. users: on its heels came another survey showing that the number of Americans who use computer on-line

services shot up in the first half of 1995 to 12 million. "On-line-services," AP (New York) 15 October 1995. Preliminary results of a 1997 survey show that forty-five percent of American households now have PCs, eighty percent of those with household incomes over $100,000 per year (*Computer Intelligence* 1998 Consumer Technology Index (CT198)).

40. See Chapters Four and Six.

41. William Gibson, *Neuromancer* (N.Y.: Berkley, 1984)

42. For an example of how vapid any discussion of these issues that avoids or ignores the underlying reality of capitalist ownership of information can be, see Anne Wells Branscomb, *Who Owns Information? From Privacy to Public Access* (N.Y.: Basic Books, 1994). After 185 pages of consideration of the question asked in her title, she concludes with breathtaking banality that "we [?] will build the kind of legal info-structure that we [?] want and need." (186)

43. James Glave, "Pentagon 'Hacker' Speaks Out," *Wired News*, 3 March 1998.

44. Rebecca Trounson, "Hacker Case Taps Into Fame, Fury," *Los Angeles Times*, 27 April 1998.

45. A survey released early in 1998 found that "64 percent of more than 500 organizations report a computer security breach within the past 12 months. That is a marked increase over 48 percent who reported breaches a year ago, and 22 percent the year before." Matt Richtel, "Study Finds Rise in Computer Crime," *New York Times*, 5 March 1998.

46. Kurt Eichenwald, "Reuters Subsidiary Target of U.S. Inquiry Into Theft of Data From Bloomberg," January 30, 1998; and Eichenwald, "Reuters Unit Puts 3 Executives on Paid Leave," *New York Times,* January 31, 1998.

47. At a conference on "Infowar," an American electronic warfare specialist told of a bizarre plan by a group of American hackers, allegedly motivated by patriotic rage at French economic espionage against the United States, to mount an "electronic assault on the main nerve centres of the French economy." Although apparently technically capable of inflicting considerable damage, the plan was called off when the FBI threatened them with arrest. "Dawn of the Infowar Era," *Intelligence Newsletter* 271 (14 September 1994) 1.

48. Matt Richtel, "New Manhattan Project Hopes To Raise Awareness of Hacking," *The New York Times*, 21 September 1997. Winn Schwartau, *Information Warfare: Cyberterrorism — Protecting your Personal Security in the Electronic Age* (Emeryville, Calif.: Thunder's Mouth Press, 1996).

49. Confidential information.

50. The state of Maryland made $12.9 million in 1996 from selling marketing firms access to its Motor Vehicle Administration data base alone. Rajiv Chandrasekaran, "Door Fling Open to Public Records," *Washington Post*, 8 March 1998.

51. Manuel Castells, *The Information Age: Economy, Society and Culture*, v. 1: *The Rise of the Network Society* (Oxford: Blackwell, 1996) 62–63.

52. Castells, 412.

53. Barnaby J. Feder, "Getting Biotechnology Set to Hatch," *New York Times*, 2 May 1998.

54. Don Tapscott, *The Digital Economy: Promise and Peril in the Age of Networked Intelligence* (N.Y.: McGraw-Hill, 1996), 12.

4—"The Night Has a Thousand Eyes": New Technologies of Surveillance

In a 1997 case that drew international attention, a young British nanny, Louise Woodward, working for a family in Massachusetts, was charged with murder in the death of an eight-month-old boy in her care. Although her conviction was overturned, in the aftermath of the highly publicized case, a new branch of the private surveillance industry put on the market "nannycams," video surveillance equipment that can be installed surreptitiously in home nurseries to record the day's activities for later secret parental inspection.[1] In advertising their new product, private security companies of course feed on their potential clients' fears, and no doubt on complex guilt feelings among some working mothers, to instill degrees of suspicion about negligence, or worse. Sophisticated new technology is involved. Tiny equipment with microvideo cameras an inch wide can be placed in teddy bears, clocks, plants, even smoke detectors. And with growing popularity, costs have fallen dramatically, putting the technology easily within reach of parents with relatively modest incomes. The video record can be relayed to a television channel specially dedicated to the purpose, or to VCR format for later review. More impressively, computer software can link cameras with a personal computer, enabling parents to take quick views in real time from their PCs at work. Another variant: a few for-profit daycares offer on-line surveillance capability on websites; working parents can thus be virtual care-giving parents through the magic of the new technology.

One of the oddities of the nannycam is the insistence on secrecy, as if it were a kind of clandestine intelligence operation. Some of the companies flogging nannycams even bear names such as Spymaster. Not surprisingly, nannies and organizations representing nannies have expressed dismay and anger at being the objects of secret videotaping. The companies seem not to have grasped the basics of panoptic logic. Under panoptic principles, it would be made crystal clear to nannies at the outset of their employment that their employers intended to have their every move watched, recorded, and analyzed. Knowing that she was being monitored continuously, she would discipline herself to behave exactly as required, to internalize the employer's rules. Perhaps in future we can expect properly panoptic nannycams. Certainly, they would have an advantage over old-fashioned Benthamite surveillance in that the new technology offers the possibility of remote operation. With on-line versions and computer mobility, parents can be inspecting in real time from wherever their work may have taken them. Is mom called away from Denver to clinch a sale or close a deal in Osaka? No problem. She can be slipping glances at nanny and baby in between sushi courses with her corporate clients. And knowing this, nanny will never relax in her performance level. Or so panoptic theory would suggest.

The nannycam is just one small example of how new technologies are transforming the electronic eye, making it pervasive and ubiquitous. Another, with far wider ramifications, is the growing use of videocams to watch over public spaces. CCTV, or closed-circuit television, has been in widespread use for some time for security purposes in spaces such as workplaces, shops, banks, apartment lobbies, parking lots, etc. Security guards manning banks of TV screens and robbery suspects caught on video are now familiar.[2] But video surveillance technology is now taking an innovative leap that is changing its hitherto limited significance. The first innovation is quantitative: the scope of electronic eyes is becoming more pervasive and overlapping. The second is qualitative: face recognition technology and the digitalization of information exchange offers the prospect of moving from the merely passive or defensive security purposes to which the technology has been largely assigned until now, into a new era of active identification and location of individuals.

A report from New York City highlights one woman's discovery of the ubiquitous electronic eye:

It had gotten so that Barbara Katende didn't even mind the cameras anymore. The ones at the courthouse she walks past every night made her feel safer. So did those at bank machines. She even accepted the ones placed in department stores to prevent shoplifting.

Then last week, Ms. Katende, 26, spotted a camera on a rooftop about 200 yards from her Kew Gardens apartment. A rooftop she had seen, but not thought about, every time she stood before her sixth-floor window with the blinds open, lounging around in her underwear. Or wrapped in a wet towel. Or in the altogether.

The camera monitors traffic at the Van Wyck Expressway-Grand Central Parkway interchange. But, as Ms. Katende learned from a reporter, it has a powerful zoom lens, can turn or tilt in any direction and is controlled by a technician in a television studio miles away in midtown Manhattan. Ms. Katende was horrified at the thought of the technician swivelling the camera toward her apartment out of boredom, or worse. "If you don't have privacy in your own house," Ms. Katende said, "you don't have privacy anywhere, do you?"[3]

High-tech peeping toms are one thing, but the proliferation of video cameras has much wider significance. The cameras have gradually been moving into more and more places in New York, quietly extending the potential visual coverage of the city. In some cases, the installation has been deliberately publicized, as with cameras trained on Washington Square Park in Greenwich Village, the first in a series of anti-crime surveillance initiatives launched by Mayor Rudolph Giuliani and his police chief.[4] But the cameras are not limited to the police, nor to government. Many are privately owned and operated, for various purposes, from security to TV traffic report monitors. The intended purposes are generally innocuous, if not benign. Critics suggest, however, that private detectives and information brokers who make their living by knowing who's who and what's what will develop sources behind the cameras. Even without a single comprehensive system in place, the patchwork of separate public and private sets of eyes will gradually begin to describe a potential surveillance network covering much of the city.

Following the lead of big cities like Baltimore that have pioneered extensive police video surveillance of known areas of criminal activity,[5] smaller centers have installed systems that are more comprehensive, due to their much smaller coverage requirements. East Newark, N.J. (population 2,000), for instance, inspired by a single violent incident, installed sixteen surveillance cameras with rotating eyes to monitor every street in the nine-block borough, twenty-four hours a day.[6] The semi-rural town of Lyons, N.Y. (population: 4,300), has installed surveillance cameras on the main streets, despite a very modest crime rate.[7] The United Kingdom has taken urban video surveillance for policing perhaps further than any other Western country. It has become relatively common in British town centers to have comprehensive street surveillance in place. The idea is catching on quickly: more than 450 towns by the end of 1997 had such systems, up from seventy-four three years earlier. There seems to be a cumulative dynamic at work: towns "without protection" fear they will become targets of criminals if they do not follow suit, and there is some evidence to this effect. This has led towns with as few of 1,500 inhabitants to get their own system. Moreover, the same dynamic seems to impel the extension of coverage once surveillance is in place, as installation of cameras increased fear of crime in side streets where there was no coverage, leading to demands for extension to residential streets and public areas.[8]

Such intensive video surveillance systems need not be merely passive, sending pictures to be manually monitored by glorified security guards. Commercial applications for automated monitoring services are now being developed and put on the market.

> Imagine that a city park were studded with discreetly placed cameras that fed images into computers programmed to keep a watchful eye. This may sound darkly Orwellian, but David Aviv, a former aerospace engineer, has patented exactly such a system as a way of combatting crime. Aviv said his invention, which he calls the Public Eye, used pattern recognition to detect robberies or acts of violence. He said he had digitized and stored a library of physical interactions. The camera sends to a computer the real-time images of a person getting money from an automated teller machine, for example. The computer then takes a snapshot and compares the image against the library of threatening interactions . . . Aviv said he also used a type of pattern recognition, called word gisting, to detect aggressive verbal interactions.[9]

The quantitative spread of video surveillance equipment is only part of the significance. New face recognition technology that is now at the experimental stage may be ready for commercial use within five years. The key, once again, is digitization. With the right software (one now under active development is called "Person Spotter"), much of it inspired by analogies to the functioning of the human brain, facial features can be reduced to a digital code. If the software is sophisticated enough, and there is no reason to think this is not achievable, such a code could be as specific in its recognition capabilities as human beings, with their remarkable pattern recognition abilities. Even a change in appearance (the addition or subtraction of facial hair, glasses, cosmetics, etc.) could be detected by software that had analyzed the features of the face in sufficient detail.[10] The advantages of automated recognition systems, of course, are the size of memory storage and speed of processing. The benefits of such "biometric" recognition systems are obvious: it will no longer be possible to steal another person's identity for purposes of fraud. A stolen credit card will be useless if the person attempting to use it is immediately identified as an imposter. Already, for instance, some automatic teller machines can scan the retina of the eye of a person using a bank card in an identification method as foolproof as fingerprinting.[11] But video analysis systems, once operational, offer much more than this. They offer the prospect of picking out a face in a crowd that matches, for instance, the face of someone flagged for attention: say, an escaped convict, a known terrorist, a deadbeat dad behind on child-support payments, or simply a missing person. This brings us back to the growing web of video surveillance in urban spaces, both public and private. If this were linked with operational video analysis systems, the technology would exist to make it very hard to hide, or to be lost. Of course, just because something is possible does not mean that it will ever happen. But even if only partially implemented, such an automated watcher system offers an ironic twist on a much voiced criticism of modern mass society — that it is so anonymous and impersonal. In the age of smart machines, guess again.

Another technological enhancement to vision is the capacity see through cover. An electromagnetic camera under development will be able to detect a weapon hidden under someone's clothing from thirty to sixty feet away. This millimeter-wave camera will take advantage of the human body's electromagnetic signals. "Colder" objects, such as guns or knives, or even plastic explosives, emit almost no such signals and essentially block the body's emissions. The camera projects a precise image of those objects on a monitor. Such cameras could be hand-held or mounted on a police cruiser; police officers could screen suspects without having to leave the safety of the squad car. Among other devices close to being operational are an x-ray imaging system that emits a very low dose of radiation that is reflected off the skin to develop, in less than a second, an electronic image of the body and everything it is carrying. Forward Looking Infrared (FLIR) technology, originally developed by the military for locating enemy aircraft, can detect very slight temperature differentials. Hand-held or vehicle-mounted mobile FLIR units can in effect "see though" walls. They may be used by patrols along the U.S.-Mexico border to detect smuggled aliens.[12] Night-vision technology, again developed in the first instance for military use, allows police to turn night into day. Danish technology for stroboscopic photocopy permits hundreds of pictures to be taken in a matter of seconds, thus allowing for all the participants in a demonstration or riot to be photographed individually.[13] Once combined with operational face recognition technology and access to global data banks, this would offer police the possibility of instant identification of individuals. Holographic projections, that could be accompanied by appropriate artificial sounds, create false visual images to confuse and disorient a target.

The advantages from a law-enforcement or security perspective of these new technologies are obvious. So are the potential threats such devices pose to citizens' privacy. Developed for one purpose, such innovations are quickly taken up for others. Many originate in military research, and are then used in police work. Even in this context, the technologies may be transferred easily from one kind of purpose to another. What is developed as an anti-crime surveillance device can be redirected against refugees, political dissidents, or striking trade unionists. Such technologies are also moving into the hands of private, corporate security, which stands outside whatever regulation and democratic accountability may constrain state agencies. Finally, new technologies inevitably make their way into the general marketplace. Recent years have seen a proliferation of shops selling personal snooping devices, no questions asked, at dramatically falling prices.

Even while remaining largely within the state sector, these new imaging technologies raise troubling questions. As a newspaper report points out:

> Some of the new weapons detectors are expected to raise novel constitutional questions about police searches, and there are no exact precedents for the answers. The millimeter-wave camera could let police officers detect weapons inside someone's clothing from across the street. Would that constitute an illegal search or would it provide probable cause to confiscate the gun? Would use of devices that can look through clothing, even though manufacturers say they do not reveal intimate details, amount to an invasion of privacy?[14]

The electronic eyes in the streets and on the rooftops cannot compare, however, to the awesome super-eyes that orbit the earth in space. Satellite reconnaissance changed the nature of the Cold War and transformed the profession of espionage. With the end of the Cold War, the 1990s have witnessed the partial declassification and commercialization of imaging technology. Scientists have begun tentative collaboration with the military-intelligence complex to draw on the vast, but largely secret, resources gathered by spy satellites for non-military research purposes, such as measuring the effects of climate change.[15] Some commercial uses are already well in place. A reporter followed a Canadian wheat farmer out on his combine one day and discovered a new element in a familiar scene:

> On a sunny day last August, Terry Gates put his John Deere combine in neutral and paused amid his 1,620 glorious hectares of wheat and barley. . . . As the motor idled, the Saskatchewan farmer inserted a data cartridge into a dashboard-mounted, 486-based computer. Seconds later, a colour display appeared on the monitor. Global Positioning System (GPS) satellites 18,000 kilometres above the Earth gave Mr. Gates his position in a wheatfield to within two metres. On the screen, among reds, greens, blues and yellows — signifying potassium distribution in the soil — he could view a graphic rendering of the six-metre strip of land on which he tested a fungicide last summer. As he hoped, his yield per bushel had increased in that tiny patch. There was a time when farmers laid wire to denote the boundaries of their land. Now wired farmers using

GPS are pushing the boundaries of what they can produce from their land.[16]

Farmers fit their combines with receivers tuned to satellites that can feed data to an on-board computer that can later be transferred to a home PC for further analysis. In the age of video surveillance, the farmer in the field is linked directly to space from whence he or she can see more and see better than on the ground.

Precision farming is based on a U.S. satellite-navigation system, the GPS that pinpoints objects on Earth by their latitude and longitude, and was used extensively in the Gulf War to direct jeeps, tanks, and missiles. GPS is matched by an equivalent Russian system, each with a full complement of twenty-four satellites circling the earth continuously broadcasting signals that can be detected from every point on the globe. A person with a receiver on the ground can pinpoint his or her location to a few meters.[17] Hikers in remote areas can, for example, check their location with hand-held sets. With future enhancements, constant monitoring of the whereabouts of, say, Alzheimer's patients or small children will be possible. As with all such technology, GPS has two sides. One is empowerment and convenience, the other is surveillance and control. It is possible, for instance, that certain individuals could be "tagged" and their location at all times tracked precisely.

As states have turned to cost recovery for their services, satellite imagery has begun to be put up for bids from the private sector. The next step was taken in 1997 with the launching of the world's first commercial spy-like satellite. "EarlyBird 1," launched atop a Russian rocket from a military base in eastern Russia, by its builder, EarthWatch Inc., of Longmont, Colorado, was supposed to end the monopoly of the world's military and intelligence services on gathering high-resolution pictures from space. To the company's chagrin, EarlyBird went mysteriously dead shortly after settling into orbit.[18] While this failure illustrates that contemporary satellite technology is by no means glitch-free, other commercial projects are following in EarlyBird's wake. Next-generation satellites in coming years will be capable of distinguishing objects on the ground with a diameter less than one meter. The U.S. government retains the right to switch off the commercial sensors in times of war or international tension. In addition, it bans U.S.-licensed satellite operators from selling images to the governments of Cuba, Libya, North Korea, Iran and Iraq, or any of their "suspected agents."[19] Presumably future launches from other nations may have fewer constraints, unless multilateral agreements are concluded to constrain the potential military exploitation of commercial satellite imagery. The problem is that satellites are "dual use" technology. Images ordered by one customer for commercial or scientific purposes might be of military use to another. Although satellite reconnaissance may have helped stabilize relations between the superpowers during the Cold War, the same technology might serve to destabilize regions in the post–Cold War era, offering belligerent or rogue states, or even sophisticated terrorist groups, the capacity to map targets for attack accurately.[20]

The commercial possibilities of spy satellites are numerous. As the British *Sunday Times* gushed: "Spy satellites, once the exclusive preserve of the security services, are to be made available to anybody with a credit card. For a few hundred pounds, it will soon be possible to see into the gardens of superstars, snoop on terrorist training camps in Libya or monitor a spouse on a business trip to Amsterdam."[21] Although commercial concerns as diverse as insurance companies and fishing trawlers have indicated potential interest in satellite imagery, a spokesperson for a civil rights group complained that "in the absence of a law of privacy there is nothing people can do to protect themselves from this sort of surveillance." Surveillance from space is out of reach of the laws of nations. If someone wants to see what is in your backyard, they would normally require your permission, or a search warrant. They need neither to take high-resolution pictures of your backyard from space.

To round out the picture of global visual surveillance, we might come down to earth again—literally. Applied research in Japan aims to create "cyberinsects," artificially enhanced and controlled insects sent on human spy missions. For instance, cockroaches have been fitted with a microcomputer "backpack" that receives remote-control signals and transmits electrical impulses to the insect's legs, guiding its direction. "Roboroaches" could be fitted with tiny cameras and microphones to search rubble for earthquake victims or spy on commercial or military rivals.[22] Military researchers have looked at developing miniaturized micro spy planes that would buzz over battlefields or enemy encampments like bees or mosquitos. It may yet be possible to be a "fly on the wall" at other people's secret meetings.

There is an old jazz song, "The Night has a Thousand Eyes." The future will have many, many more eyes than that. What is more, with digital data technology and globally networked real-time communications, the potential for sharing this information is truly awesome. For instance, tracking systems to follow particular individuals as they move in and out of range of local surveillance grids could be directed from satellites, offering what amounts to global coverage. Granted, there is no global Big Brother on the immediate horizon with the clout to put all this together, but even discontinuous and haphazard visual webs can add up to total coverage beyond the wildest dreams of Jeremy Bentham, with his pre-technological Inspector peering with the unaided eye at his tiny ring of cells.

It was a vertiginous moment for humanity when the Apollo space mission to the moon in 1969 sent back pictures of earth as seen from space. For the first time we saw our home, ourselves, from the outside, as it were. Some have hoped this will encourage a more global ecological conception of our planet. Ironically, that same image can be understood as the beginning of another vertiginous reversal of perspective—this time with the whole earth as the object of the self-reflexive, panoptic eye.

"I HEAR YOU":
THE GLOBAL WALLS HAVE EARS

Wiretaps and bugs have been staples of security and intelligence operations. Nobody can read another's mind, but a great deal of information about people's motives and intentions can be derived from intercepted verbal communications—especially when those communications are believed to be private.

In most Western countries laws regulate the use of wiretaps or bugs by police and security forces. Such controls are patchy at best, as considerations of national security and law and order usually prevail over concerns about civil liberties. But patchy and erratic as they have proven in practice, they are increasingly becoming outmoded by technological advances that have outstripped the capacity regulations to describe adequately the behavior and techniques to be regulated. Most regulation of wiretaps, for instance, is premised on the existence of a physical intervention, a "tap" placed on a wire that picks up and records voice communication over that wire. Bugs are understood as physical objects, planted surreptitiously onto an unsuspecting host, like microphones secretly placed inside walls, or covertly carried by one person to record what someone else says.

This sort of old-fashioned eavesdropping continues, on a very large scale. Indeed, improved technology means that anyone willing to spend relatively modest amounts of money can purchase sophisticated, highly sensitive camouflaged listening and recording devices. Bugging is no longer the prerogative of the FBI or the DEA. It can now be used by jealous spouses, suspicious business partners, or simply someone with a prurient interest in other peoples'' activities. A recent example is Special Prosecutor Kenneth Starr's "wiring" Linda Tripp to record her supposedly private conversation with Monica Lewinsky in a bar, a conversation which was then used to precipitate a scandal that, momentarily at least, threatened to result in the impeachment of the President of the United States. And just as the Louise Woodward case triggered nannycam sales, bugging-equipment suppliers understand the Tripp incident as a "billboard" advertising their products. Washington, "with lots of lawyers, deal-making and mistrust" has long been a prime market for do-it-yourself buggers. "Thank God for paranoia in our business. It's fabulous," said one Internet surveillance equipment salesman.[23] Business has been at the center of much of the bugging activity but there is also growing interest in the listening devices for other reasons. Concealed microphones are used by police officers to record their encounters with suspects; workers trying to prove sexual harassment; parents checking up on their kids; and suspicious husbands and wives. All good news for the private surveillance business. Bugging technology has particularly excelled in miniaturization. The legendary olive in the martini glass that doubles as a mini-microphone may be a bit of a James Bond fantasy, but other devices as astonishingly tiny and largely undetectable are available to just about anyone willing to pay.

The physical placement of a listening device is no longer necessary to intercept a conversation. Laser technology permits a highly concentrated beam to be directed at a window from a remote location, the only requirement being an unobstructed line between the laser device and the target. The laser beam is ultra-sensitive to vibrations on the window pane caused by any sounds inside the room, and transmits this information instantly back to the listeners. Moreover, through the magic of digitization, extraneous noise can simply be removed, leaving only the conversation being targeted, in much the same way that old vinyl records are digitally remastered on compact disk format to exclude the hisses, pops, scratches and other surface noises that once marred the original recording. Thus, traditional counter-surveillance measures—flushing the toilet, say, or playing loud music to drown out the words—will be useless. Indeed, it is technically possible for a recorded conversation to be stored in a purer, clearer form than what the participants actually heard at the time.

Intercepting private face-to-face conversations remains an important aspect of surveillance. But in the world in which we now live, face-to-face conversations will likely make up only a portion, a rather small portion, of the significant verbal communications in which people are involved. The telephone as a globally popular extension of the human voice has always been a target for listening in, hence the wiretap. But less and less telephone traffic is carried over wire. Intercity and intercontinental long distance, a huge growth area in telecommunications, is bounced off communications satellites, or transmitted by microwave relay. In metropolitan areas, even intracity volume often overloads the antiquated wiring system, causing calls to be automatically shunted to the satellite system. Thus a staggering volume of telephone traffic exists in the form of electromagnetic impulses in the ether. These can be scooped out of the air and read without any old-fashioned physical intervention like a wiretap. Not only can this be done, it is being done.

The Intelsat communications satellite system is used to relay most of the world's phone calls, faxes, telexes, Internet, and e-mail communications around the globe. Paralleling this network of satellite coverage is a highly secretive shadow network of listening posts and tracking stations, organized by Western intelligence agencies that intercept and monitor all communications relayed by Intelsat. This is the UKUSA network, so called because of the still-secret agreements in the early stages of the Cold War, between the U.S. National Security Agency (NSA) and the British Government Communications Headquarters (GCHQ) as the chief partners, and the NSA clearly the senior partner on the basis of superior U.S. resources; a second level of junior partners, including Canada, Australia, and New Zealand; and a further, outer ring of countries who cooperate with the alliance, by, for example, allowing listening posts to be installed on their territory. The original purpose of UKUSA was signals intelligence in the context of the Cold War. Every square foot of the Soviet bloc was blanketed for interception and decryption of military and political communications.[24] In the aftermath of the Cold War, there was no question of closing down this global high-tech investment. The strategically placed vacuum cleaners in the sky keep right on sucking up the world's telecommunications, despite misgiving from critics and even some defectors from the agencies themselves.[25] They even tap into land-based telecommunications systems, thus completing near-total coverage of the world's communications.

The mere capacity to intercept communications in the world on any given day would be, in and of itself, more than useless. Indeed, it would quickly turn these agencies into latter-day equivalents of the sorcerer's apprentice. What makes the interception capacities interesting is that sophisticated computer software programs now permit electronic flagging of communications. A vast amount of "noise" is sorted to yield a small number of significant "signals." Just as commercial search engines crawl quickly over the Internet, returning with multiple matches for search terms entered, the daily volume of communications traffic can be searched to turn up specific items of interest, the little gold nuggets in the tidal wave of dross. Keyword recognition capabilities can be triggered by words, phrases or by the addresses of specific senders or receivers. A great deal of research is going into voice recognition technology to enable people to talk to their computers. We can rest assured that voice recognition software will first be used as one more sorting device separating the wheat from the chaff.

In 1996, New Zealand investigative journalist and activist Nicky Hager published a remarkably detailed book on New Zealand's role in the signals intelligence network that revealed for the first time ever the existence of a globally integrated communications intelligence system codenamed ECHELON. Clearly under American leadership, ECHELON links all the computers among the cooperating UKUSA agencies using a set of keywords. "Under the ECHELON system, a particular station's Dictionary computer contains not only its parent agency's chosen keywords, but also a list for each of the other four agencies . . . So each station collects all the telephone calls, faxes, telexes, Internet messages and other electronic communications that its computers have been pre-programmed to select for all the allies and automatically sends this intelligence to them."[26] Each of the agencies has always denied that they turn their spying capacity inward on their own citizens. It has been alleged that they might turn to each other for domestic spy jobs. ECHELON makes it clear that no such specific requests are necessary: the entire process is automated in such a way that borders become irrelevant.

There are a number of points to make about this communications intelligence system. First, it is indisputably to the greatest benefit to the United States, which takes the dominant role in setting the search terms. Junior partners such as Canada, Australia, and New Zealand get relatively limited benefits in exchange for their participation. Much of the world is left out altogether. What use is being made of intercepts, and for what purposes? With the end of the Cold War, the anti-Communist consensus that animated the alliance for four decades is irrelevant. There is much talk of counterterrorism, the threat of transnational organized crime and economic concerns. Critics worry that American national interests are being served under the cloak of global security. I return to these issues in the last chapter. For now, it is enough to note that in the world of communications intelligence, it is states, and mainly the world's only real superpower, the United States, that play the preponderant role in communications interception. So far the system is too complex and sophisticated for individuals or even organized groups to make any serious use of it. And it should also be noted that technological innovation in transmission may also run ahead of the capacity of even the high-tech spy agencies for interception. As transmission of data shifts to fiber optic cable, which has huge potential as a carrier for the information age, the eavesdropping agencies may find their sources drying up. I have myself heard people from these agencies lamenting their inability to intercept fiber optic transmissions, forcing them to intercept at the receiving end — a messier and more complicated task. The same resourceful agencies have also developed TEMPEST technology that allows them to read from a distance computer communications and even files on computer hard drives from the electromagnetic radiation emitted.[27]

Some innovations in telecommunications have also made interception easier. A case in point are the mobile cellular phones that have become a familiar part of business and personal communication in the past few years. A new generation of commercial satellite systems will carry telephone communications, making it possible for cell phone users to reach anyone anywhere on the earth.[28] Such global wireless technology is enormously convenient, but cell phones constitute a notorious security risk. U.S. House Speaker Newt Gingrich learned this to his chagrin when a Florida couple picked up and taped a cellular phone conversation between an Ohio Congressman, Gingrich, and other Republicans, including the majority leader in the House. The conversation took place on the same day Gingrich admitted that he had violated House ethics rules by failing to obtain adequate legal advice on the use of tax-exempt money and then providing inaccurate information during the investigation of the matter. During the call, the speaker and his colleagues discussed how to handle the political fallout from the ethics charges. A partial transcript of the conversation was published in the *New York Times*. Democrats complained that the call had violated an agreement Gingrich made with the Committee on Standards of Official Conduct. Republicans complained about violation of privacy. The couple said that they had taped the call "because they thought it was historic."[29] Sophisticated cell phone listening devices, which are available commercially and can, for instance, simultaneously record conversations on multiple tracks as well as locate the geographical position of the callers, fall into a very grey legal area in the United States. Government and telecommunications companies buy these products, but they may also find their way into the hands of drug traffickers, organized criminals, and terrorists, who can use them against law-enforcement agencies. In California, a federal prosecution was launched against a company selling such equipment in what amounted to a sting operation. Ironically, part of the government's evidence was based on intercepted cell phone calls.[30] There is an inherent problem with legally enforcing a government and corporate monopoly over technology that is already cheap and widely available. It is probably sensible for anyone using a cell phone to assume that someone—the police, the Mafia, a jealous spouse, or just a voyeur on the street—*might* be listening in.

Bad enough that anyone can listen in on cell phone calls, but it has also become known that a cell phone can be used to monitor the location of the person carrying it. As long as it is turned on, it can periodically emit a signal that is sent to a central company location. Conversely, the monitoring can be centralized, emanating outward from a central location and detecting and positioning all cell phones within the network. Already in the United Kingdom, cell phone-tracking data are being retained for a two-year period and have been made available to law-enforcement agencies. One murder conviction has been attributed to such tracking evidence. In the United States, proposed federal regulations have, typically, been prompted by an eminently practical need: to have available 911 emergency service for mobile phones with pinpoint location to guide emergency response teams to the site of the call. However, civil libertarians are still suspicious of the interest that the FBI has shown in a centralized tracking system. As the senior staff counsel at the Center for Democracy and Technology, a civil liberties group, explained, the technology contains an inherent paradox: "Law enforcement is right that this technology may help track kidnappers, but it's also going to help the kidnappers stalk their victims."[31]

"NEVER LEAVE HOME WITHOUT IT": ELECTRONIC TAGS TO SMART CARDS

We have looked at the eyes and ears of the new panoptic technologies. Another set of techniques, closely related to these, is electronic identification devices. As befits panoptic technology, many of these techniques were developed for use by prisons. Electronic tags for paroled prisoners are an example. Such tags emit a signal that monitors the parolee's location and notifies the authorities if he moves out of the area to which he is limited. This procedure has been employed throughout North America to mixed reviews.[32] The practice is also on the increase in the United Kingdom, where electronic monitoring of community service is seen as a cheaper alternative to incarceration.[33] This could be seen as an extension of the panoptic power of the prison beyond its physical boundaries. But just as typically, other, less apparently coercive forms of the same identification technology are being introduced in the wider society.

Credit, banking, and other personal ID cards are meant to offer convenience and security. Yet, slowly but surely, they are being transformed into an equivalent to electronic tags, electronic IDs that can locate and track individuals. Workplace ID cards, increasingly used by large organizations, both public and private, begin as, and in many cases remain, little more than pieces of plastic with a picture and perhaps a signature. A security guard may scan these and match the face against the bearer at an entry point, and it may be required that individuals carry the ID in some prominent place at all times on the premises. This is crude, but probably effective for most security purposes. New technologies offer a number of enhancements that are initially expensive but nonetheless attractive to employers. Smart ID cards encode unique information, such as finger or palm prints or retina patterns. Equipment can automatically scan the card and its holder to check for a match. Other identification marks might in future include face or voice recognition, or even "DNA fingerprinting." But the uses of smart ID cards do not stop at the company gates. Inside, a monitoring system can track and locate everyone at all times. Smart buildings could also ensure automatic channeling of employees within prescribed locations: employees might be authorized for access to some but not all parts of the building depending on their function and status, and their cards would contain that information in machine-readable form. The security advantages for employers are obvious, although it should be pointed out that these advantages might also be appreciated by employees concerned about their personal safety, such as women working late hours. But the advantages for employers do not stop with security. Smart IDs also permit monitoring of performance, enabling employers to record, for instance, just how much time an employee takes in the coffee shop or the washroom.

Smart credit, debit, cash, and other banking cards offer less obvious routes to a general tracking and surveillance regime. "Dumb" cards already leave behind a recorded trail. A monthly credit card statement is a record of where its owner has shopped and what he or she has purchased, and sometimes a travel itinerary as well. But such trails can also be misleading, as cards can be lost or stolen, and misuse is fairly easy. In fact, police in various countries have uncovered large scams involving forged or stolen credit card numbers, amounting to billions of dollars in losses. To take just one incident, a San Francisco hacker snuck into a major Internet provider, collected 100,000 credit card numbers and tried to sell the credit information, according to the FBI. He allegedly inserted a program that gathered the credit information from a dozen companies selling products over the Internet. Unfortunately for him, he tried to sell the credit information, which he encrypted, to an undercover FBI agent for $260,000.[34] Technology such as that employed in smart weapons to find and destroy enemy targets is being used by the banking industry to zero in on credit card thieves. Computers build and analyze spending profiles of individual cardholders. The software, called Falcon, learns to recognize patterns by looking at large numbers of transactions. "In its defense applications, computers have been taught to recognize visual profiles of potential targets, such as enemy tanks. The system allows pilots and ground troops to fire in the direction of an enemy outside their range of vision, and depend on the missile to find and destroy the target." The same logic is applied to credit card fraud. Profiles of credit card misuse are drawn up and matched against actual transactions. Suspicious or anomalous patterns can be pinpointed for closer investigation. In addition to computer intelligence, investigators have "tapped into a worldwide computer network originally created for the U.S. government . . . [to build] a secure database through which members can share information about suspected fraud rings and their techniques."[35]

Smarter credit cards that verify that the user is indeed the authorized card holder are clearly in the interests of both companies and card holders, and as recognition technologies become cheaper and diffused more widely, pressure will increase to embed chips with more personal identification data. As the trend toward a cashless society intensifies, verifiable smart cards will leave more comprehensive trails. Moreover, such cards offer the additional possibility of building ever more detailed profiles of their owners' buying preferences and even their habitual behavior patterns (when and where they tend to shop, when they travel and to where, etc.). And this information can flow backward to the credit card company or forward to the merchant accepting the card, if the law permits such data to be transferred and the merchant is willing to purchase access to their customers' consumer profiles. Another possibility is to use fingerprinting to verify the identity of anyone using a credit card number to transact business over the Net. Fingerprints of users would be scanned and matched against the fingerprint record held by the card company. One technique already on the market embeds fingerprint recognition in the user's own keyboard. As you type, your fingerprints are being relayed across the Net.[36] The implications of this for law-enforcement surveillance are intriguing, to say the least. Although competition between cards would seem to complicate the emergence of a global tracking capacity, electronic data matching can easily build up what amounts to comprehensive coverage. This possibility is discussed in greater detail in the next chapter.

The potential of smart cards has interested governments as well as corporations. A universal personal identification card would protect states against abuse of various social and welfare services and simplify and reduce the cost of a number of bureaucratic tasks. Already Social Security numbers and their equivalents serve this purpose in a number of countries. One cannot earn money legally without providing the number, nor can one access government services. Through them, a profile of certain characteristics of individual citizens is automatically amassed, in taxation and social services records, etc. In 1996, Lexis-Nexis, a Dayton, Ohio-based information broker, granted easy on-line access to consumer Social Security numbers for a brief period. As part of its "Person Locator" service, clients could search the company's data base for millions of individuals' Social Security numbers. Lexis-Nexis officials said they had "expected clients to use the service to locate witnesses and heirs, or to track down suspected criminals." Social Security numbers were up for grabs for ten days before public pressure forced the service to be shut down. The U.S. Social Security administration itself has a website, designed to be a service for people seeking updates and estimates on future benefits, that for a time provided detailed information about individuals' personal income and retirement benefits. "Privacy advocates were up in arms, saying the site could easily be misused by ex-spouses, landlords, employers, co-workers, credit agencies, and lookup services." Bowing to pressure, the administration shut down the site in question, saying that it would consider bringing it back only with expanded security features, including basic password protection.[37]

Irrespective of commercial misuse, government can readily combine and match data from its own various banks. Because of Big Brother imagery associated with the state, especially in North America, government ID cards raise more hackles among the public than the more apparently decentralized private sector. It will probably take a long time for North America to come to a universal smart card ID. But in the United Kingdom, the Labour government has raised the issue where its Conservative predecessor had backed off. They are being considered as "part of a package of measures to improve public services." The cards would be voluntary but ministers "hope everyone will choose to carry one," in light of the benefits the cards would offer.[38] Pressures toward adoption of universal personal IDs, and toward smarter electronic versions thereof, will likely increase in the near future to the point where they become practically irresistible.

The advantages of such IDs are glaring to states that are increasingly cost-conscious and eager to protect the diminishing amounts spent on social services and public welfare in these days of neoliberal dominance in public agenda-setting. But in an era of globalization, pressures for smarter IDs will come from outside as well as within. International travel and migration appear as both requirements of a global economy and potential threats to security. Business and professional travellers and migrants are the lifeblood of the global economy, but movements of terrorists, drug traffickers, transnational criminals, money launderers, etc., as well as large and volatile movements of political and economic refugees, undermine the workings of the "legitimate" transnational economy. At the moment, passports are issued in machine-readable form according to international agreement. These are scanned at airport check-in counters and immigration controls, and automatically call up a computer file corresponding to the name on the passport. In most cases, no traces occur, but a minority are flagged for a variety of reasons and the holders may be detained or denied permission to travel. Ticketing information on international air travel is held in a common data base to which all carriers have access. This is a convenience to air travellers as it facilitates arrangements for alternate connections when flights are cancelled or missed. It is not well known that this data base is routinely accessed by the NSA in the United States, from whence it can be made available to other U.S. intelligence and policing agencies. Thus the NSA has access to global tracking of the movement of persons by air to set beside its global access to telecommunications. The problem, however, lies in stolen, forged, or otherwise falsified passports and travel documents. The NSA can tell at any moment which travel documents are in transit between countries, but it can perhaps be less certain about the persons carrying these documents. With universal acceptance of smart card personal identification technologies—admittedly, a long way off at the moment—each passport would be uniquely linked to the verifiable personal characteristics of its holder. At that point, a true global tracking regime would fall into place. And with it, of course, a series of potential constraints on individual freedoms.

WHEN THE SCREEN LOOKS BACK AT YOU:
SEARCH ENGINES AND COOKIES

There has been a great deal of enthusiasm for the "empowerment" offered by the Internet to individuals and groups. Some of the political questions raised by this are addressed later.[39] And, in fact, the new information technologies do enable and empower people. So did earlier information technologies. The printing press undermined the Papacy and assisted the spread of the Protestant Reformation, and encouraged individualism, the emergence of an urban bourgeoisie and the rise of scientific humanism.[40] The telephone drastically reduced the limitations imposed by distance. Radio and, even more, television opened up access to worlds hitherto remote. Yet each innovation had another side. Print liberated but print was also censored. Books were banned and burned. Telephones were tapped. Radio and TV could be instruments of education but also of propaganda.

New information technologies are two-sided. They enable and empower, but they make their users more vulnerable to surveillance and manipulation. The two sides cannot be separated: it is precisely what empowers that also extends vulnerability. Cyberspace is no exception. Going on-line lets you communicate with other people on-line anywhere on the globe. Being on-line may also mean that everything you communicate might be read and traced back to its source. It might mean that persons or groups might be building an on-line profile of you—which sites you visit, which advertisements you click on, which products you order, which newsgroups you subscribe to, which e-mail addresses you correspond with. It might mean that your credit card number is stolen and misused. It might even mean that, via the Net, persons unknown to you invade your computer hard drive, look at what is there, perhaps even change or erase files, or plant a virus. Of course, none of these things may ever happen. But they could.

Among the wonderful advantages of the Internet to users are the search engines that trawl the Web to bring back multiple matches to search terms entered. For instance, in writing this book, I have occasionally required a particular reference or quotation whose source I did not have at hand. Once upon a time, a writer in this position would have to search his or her shelves for a book that might contain the reference; failing that, a time-consuming trip to a library would be in order. With the Internet, search time can be compressed dramatically, and one need travel no further than one's computer. Moreover, the service is absolutely free, and I can download the quotation into my computer and then instantly paste it into my own text where required. This is empowering technology.

But precisely the same search power can be turned around and used for less benign purposes. Try this: If you have ever given out your telephone number to a stranger—and who has not, for example, when doing business over the phone?—go to an AT&T website called www.anywho.com, type in your number, and then read back detailed information about your location, including a map to your home. An instant data base for cyber-stalkers. There is a great deal of personal information on the web that can be searched for reasons of curiosity, commercial gain, or more sinister motives. Information brokers who offer expert searches often are able to gain entry to restricted data which a private searcher might find difficult or impossible to access.[41] Private eyes have come a long way from the old Raymond Chandler gumshoe image of the past; today they may be more likely to be surfing the Net for the information to nail an unfaithful spouse or a cheating business partner. Similarly, criminals are as likely to be cruising cyberspace looking for victims as cruising back alleys.

Not surprisingly, to preempt potential government regulation, the Information Technology Industry Council, a consortium of private information brokers and credit-reporting companies, has introduced a set of "principles" or "guidelines" for the protection of Net "consumers." The principles are entirely voluntary, with no provisions for enforcement.[42] Individuals would have to "opt out" by positively indicating to the participating companies that they wish to have their personal information be kept out of data bases with public access. Critics point out that most people do not even know that such data bases exist.[43] This arrangement was undertaken with the blessing of the U.S. Federal Trade Commission and the Clinton administration, and "sets in motion the first meaningful trial of the Clinton administration's privacy policy, the stated goal of which is to protect individual privacy in the Internet age without resorting to new laws and regulations." The FTC plans a survey of 1,200 commercial websites "to gauge the effect of self-regulated approaches to consumer privacy," and will report to Congress.[44] Typically, however, the "let the market regulate itself" orientation of the Clinton administration goes only so far. There was a tradeoff involved in this agreement. It also gives law-enforcement agencies easy access to the same data bases. Traditionally, the government and courts have placed limits on the ease with which police officials can collect certain types of information on citizens without subpoenas.[45] In the age of cyberspace, industry self-regulation allows law enforcement to get around the guidelines set to protect privacy.

The search capacities of the Net hardly exhaust the technological basis for surveillance of Net activities. Among the more interesting cyber-surveillance techniques are "cookies." Net users who register with sites or download software have cookies placed directly on their hard drives. Cookies are strings of numbers that identify the user to the merchant. They speed up the process of doing business. For instance, if I register to subscribe to a service, a cookie implanted in my computer automatically re-registers me each time I enter the site, obviating a time-consuming process of entering identification and remembering a password. For this reason, they are popular with users. They are even more popular with site owners because a cookie can encode information about the user gathered at the time of initial registration, or potentially expanded with information from other sites, through links based on the user's identification. However convenient, cookies can be downright poisonous—they are a key to gaining remote access to personal computer hard drives, with frightening potential for abuse.[46] As awareness of the potential dangers of cookies has risen, various defenses have been made available. "Cookie cruncher" programs remove cookies from a hard drive. And Net browsers like Netscape give users the option to refuse all cookies, or to be warned in advance that an action will initiate a cookie, or to be warned each time an existing cookie is about to be activated. Most users, however, even if they might reject a cookie from a dubious source, will likely opt for ease of operation most of the time. I tried using the option to give specific assent to any cookie about to be activated — the experiment lasted less than a day, until I could no longer put up with constant warning messages flashing on the screen, and opted for less safety but greater ease. That is in a sense a paradigm of the empowerment/ surveillance dilemma posed by Internet technology.

@ WIT'S END: E-MAIL SURVEILLANCE

E-mail is at the heart of the popularity of the Internet as a communications technology. E-mail is rapidly becoming far and away the most used system for interpersonal and interorganizational communication in the developed world, supplanting "snail mail," as the old postal system is derisively termed. Even the fax, which experienced a rapid rise to ubiquity in businesses and home offices, is declining as users realize that even lengthy documents can instantly be transferred as attachments from computer to computer or from network to network anywhere in the world via e-mail. E-mail exemplifies the empowering capacity of the Internet, virtually abolishing spatial and time constraints on communication. In the near future, this technology may begin to come together with telephone communication, resulting in a hybrid in which real-time voice and text may be carried together, even in the same message.[47]

That said, e-mail is a most insecure form of communication. Unauthorized mail-opening is widely prohibited by law and, it must be said, generally condemned by most people as an infringement of privacy. In wartime and in emergency conditions, governments have insisted upon mail censorship, and many governments do use it as an occasional weapon in law enforcement, in which case it is usually constrained by various stipulations and procedural caveats. However, the very ease with which e-mail zips around the globe has transformed the notion of communicative relationships. As the cryptographer Whitfield Diffie has noted in a statement to Congress: "No right of private conversation was enumerated in the Constitution. I suppose it never occurred to anyone at the time that it could be prevented. Now, however, we are on the verge of a world in which electronic communication is both so good and so inexpensive that intimate business and personal relationships will flourish between parties who can at most occasionally afford the luxury of travelling to visit each other. If we do not accept the right of these people to protect the privacy of their communication, we take a long step in the direction of a world in which privacy will belong only to the rich."[48]

There is very little constraint on surveillance, both public and private, of e-mail, despite its increasing importance. At the governmental level, we have already noted that the UKUSA communications intelligence network through its ECHELON program intercepts much of the traffic bounced off the communications satellite systems. But that is only part of the problem. Internet service providers may archive incoming and outgoing e-mail traffic. Employers may not only archive e-mail within company networks, but also may insist on the right to read what employees are saying: after all, the computers and the network are company property, and what is done on these networks may be considered company business. Amitai Etzioni, the noted sociologist and communitarian philosopher, citing court rulings and the lack of federal or state legislative protection, complains that "an employee's right to e-mail privacy has little or no legal foundation." With surveys suggesting that more than a third of corporations regularly monitor their employees electronically, using techniques including e-mail spot-checks, Etzioni argues, employers are undermining any sense of community in the workplace.[49] There is another side to this issue as well. Governments and employers clearly have a legitimate interest in making sure that the communication systems they are providing are not being used for criminal and unethical purposes. And indeed, women and racial minorities have made claims for protection from sexually harassing or racist messages circulated by other employees to intimidate them. Finally, there may sometimes be a public interest in access to e-mail used for unlawful or corrupt purposes. It was archived e-mail correspondence that sank Col. Oliver North and other conspirators in the Iran-Contra affair.[50]

One of the more worrisome aspects of e-mail interception is that both the sender and recipient can be identified and located through their e-mail addresses, the ubiquitous "@." Concern about this vulnerability has led some users to seek out systems that might guarantee anonymity from prying eyes. "Re-mailing" systems are an example. A sender routes his or her e-mail messages through a remailer, who scrubs out any identifying marks from the message that could identify and locate the sender before sending it on, and then re-routes return messages. To someone concerned about privacy, that sounds like a good idea. To governments and intelligence and law-enforcement agencies, however, re-mailers sound like a screen for nefarious communications, from drug-trafficking instructions to terrorist planning. Allegations have been made, though not independently verified, that intelligence and law-enforcement agencies in a number of Western countries, including the United States, have adopted a classic counterintelligence tactic and taken control of a number of re-mailer services.[51] If there is any truth to these allegations, what purport to be services guaranteeing anonymity to clients may in fact be government surveillance operations. Whatever the facts, one thing is clear: e-mail, however empowering, is an inherently insecure method of communication. That leads us to the very large question of encryption on the Internet. If it seems more or less inescapable that governments, employers, and other corporate bodies will intercept and monitor e-mail, then perhaps the trick will be to make e-mail unreadable to anyone but the intended recipient.

THE WIZARD WAR ON THE WEB: ENCRYPTION, DECRYPTION, TRAP DOORS

As mentioned in an earlier chapter,[52] one of the great triumphs of Allied intelligence during World War II was their capacity to break Axis codes and read their military communications. This application of advanced mathematical skills to the puzzle of enemy codes was part of what Sir Winston Churchill referred to admiringly as the "wizard war." The successes of Bletchley Park in the United Kingdom in opening the "Ultra" intelligence and of the United States "Magic" decryption of the Japanese codes were only one dramatic chapter in the race between encryption and decryption techniques. But the weak link in cryptography was always that both the sender and the receiver of encrypted messages needed the same "key" used to unscramble the data. This could only be done by advance agreement or by couriers carrying keys back and forth. Hence the spy gear of codebooks, once only pages, or machines such as the German "Enigma," which, once in the hands of the enemy, could be analyzed and mastered. A Soviet code book that fell into the hands of the Americans during the war led, after years of analysis, to the "Venona" decrypts of Soviet communications with their spy networks in the United States and to the identification of Soviet atomic espionage agents. More recently, it has been alleged that the National Security Agency had for decades a secret agreement with Crypto AG, a Swiss company that sold cryptography technology to many countries and commercial concerns, allowing the NSA and its leading intelligence allies complete access to supposedly secret communications.[53]

Security of communication in cyberspace progressed by a huge leap in the 1970s with a profound advance in cryptography called "public-key encryption." Unlike the symmetrical cryptography where sender and receiver use the same key, public-key cryptography is asymmetrical, using two related keys: a public key and a private key. It is computationally infeasible to derive the private key from the public key. A public-key system is one in which the intended recipients of encrypted messages can alone read them. Possession of the public key does not, however, permit anyone other than the authorized holder of the private key to unlock the information. The private key is a mathematical value, or algorithm, sometimes called a trap door. If known, this value will unlock the communication, but if not known, the trap door remains shut, and the message remains unreadable. A layperson's description of how this operates is provided by Ashley Dunn in the *New York Times*:

> Alice . . . has a safe deposit box that has two keys. One key, which Alice always keeps as a private key, can only open the box; the other key, which is copied and widely distributed as a public key, can only lock it. When Bob . . . wants to send a message to Alice, he grabs a public lock key, places his message in the open safety deposit box and then locks it. When Alice wants to read the message, she opens the box with her private key and leaves the box open. Thus only Alice can read, but anyone can send.[54]

There is recent evidence that the idea of public-key encryption was first "discovered," if that is the correct word, by British cryptographers working at the GCHQ, the peacetime successor agency to wartime Bletchley Park (although the NSA may have been working on similar ideas even earlier, in the early 1960s.) Feeling constrained by secrecy in the interests of national security, the GCHQ cryptographers never made their discovery public.[55] Two American cryptographers unaffiliated with the secret state, Martin Hellman and Whitfield Diffie, published the concept of public-key encryption in a landmark paper in 1976. A year later, three other researchers put the concept into practice by coming up with a specific one-way trap-door function called the RSA algorithm.

Public-key encryption means the end of the state's monopoly and the democratization of encryption. Various software encryption packages are on the market—the best known being PGP, or "Pretty Good Privacy," which uses a sophisticated 128-bit system that may very well be uncrackable by even the most advanced computers. By contrast, the current U.S. government standard, DES, a 56-bit key system, was broken in thirty-nine days, as a kind of sporting challenge, by a coordinated team of computer programmers and enthusiasts.[56] One-hundred-twenty-eight–bit systems are exponentially more complex than 56-bit systems. With programs such as PGP on the market, the prospect opens that every Internet user could secure his or her communications from the prying eyes of competitors, enemies, and even the state.

There are very powerful lobbies for strong encryption. Business on the Net has never come near to realizing the potential seen for it by its enthusiasts. One of the problems is public concern about the security of financial information, such as credit card numbers, used to transact business on the Net. Encryption that had public confidence would change that. So would biometric recognition techniques such as direct electronic fingerprinting over the Net. Another issue is corporate concern over the protection of intellectual property, obviously a major problem in the age of instant digital transmission. Employing a version of public-key encryption, five giants of the computer and electronics industries, including Intel and Sony, have agreed on ways to prevent people from making illicit copies of copyrighted digital content. "The agreement marks a promising new step in the often delicate dance between creators of content—such as movies, music and books—and new technologies, such as the Internet, that make it easier both to distribute their works and pirate them."[57]

Governments do not like public-key encryption. The U.S. government in particular, given its hegemonic role as the world's only remaining superpower and closest thing to a global policeman, is especially hostile to public-key encryption. The Clinton administration has fought a series of legislative battles to try to assert its control over this technology. It began with ham-handed attempts to impose the so-called "clipper chip," an electronic trap door controlled by the government. The clipper chip failed, but the administration has insisted on strict export controls over public-key encryption packages, and has redoubled its efforts to bring about legislative requirements for government-controlled trap doors on all privacy packages sold in the United States, or what has been called public-key escrow. The government's position, reiterated on any number of occasions by the director of the FBI, is that public-key encryption will allow organized crime or terrorist groups to keep law-enforcement agencies from learning of their plans. The same FBI, it might be noted, has also insisted on technology standards in new telephone equipment that will permit the agency to continue to wiretap at will.

There are a number of hugely significant issues wrapped up within this story, the outcome of which is not yet known. On the one hand, it might appear to be a classic question of individual rights versus national security, with the same arguments deployed by the same players as in arguments about wiretaps, bugs, or human sources planted by police or security forces. Yet this similarity is superficial. The technology of public-key encryption is altogether different from conventional countersurveillance measures. It appears to be able, if unimpeded by imposed government trap doors, to secure communications effectively for long enough to render decryption capabilities irrelevant for most purposes. Even if future decryption techniques were dramatically improved, 128-bit encryption is so complex that decryption would take long enough to meet most people's privacy concerns—and certainly long enough for criminals or terrorists to carry out their plans. Moreover, the availability already of such encryption presents a genie-out-of-the-bottle problem: whatever controls might be imposed in the future, the technology would already be out there and in the hands of anyone who wanted to use it, or to distribute it illegally (hardly a problem in the age of the Internet and digital data transfer). Export controls by the U.S. government would appear to be a doomed strategy appropriate to an age when national borders and customs controls could stop the transnational movement of goods and services. Nor have American exhortations to other governments been very effective in obtaining similar action within their national jurisdictions. The Electronic Privacy Information Center, a Washington-based research group, found in a survey of 243 governments that the United States is virtually the only democratic industrialized nation seeking domestic regulation of strong encryption.[58] In the absence of a global control regime, there is no stopping the spread of strong public-key encryption. A final argument against a government trap door is that those with the motive to avoid government scrutiny would evade such controls; for the law-abiding citizens and organizations who accepted the rules, the state's monopoly of trap doors could itself become a major security problem. What if security risks or corrupt officials within the government provided the secrets to criminal or terrorist groups or to hostile states? Significant portions of the communications and computer systems in the United States could be thus opened to devastating cyber-attack. President Clinton's Commission on Critical Infrastructure Protection, while echoing the administration's line on key escrow, also suggests that the best form of national security might well be strong encryption systems that would render the nation's informational infrastructure invulnerable to assault.[59]

It would seem that in this battle, only one side can eventually win. The U.S. government's position is theoretically dubious, and impossible to police effectively in practice. Consequently, it seems more likely that widespread diffusion of strong encryption will win out eventually. While this offers protection to criminal and terrorist elements, it also offers widespread protection to individuals, groups, and organizations from the threat of intrusion from either state or non-state interests. Given the awesome technological capacities for intrusive surveillance we have been looking at, this kind of decentralized, democratic security may be the best option.

LITTLE BROTHER AND NET-NANNY: CENSORSHIP IN CYBERSPACE

Encryption provides security for communications in cyberspace. But the security of the content of private e-mails is one thing. What is said and made available on the Internet has raised an entirely different set of issues around censorship. There has, in fact, been a degree of public panic about the threat posed by the Internet to morals and safety, especially with regard to pornography and hate propaganda. The Internet as a vehicle for political subversion has been less a concern in Western countries than in the Third World, and will be looked at later.[60] Alarms about pornography and racist propaganda have been sounded loudly throughout the West and a series of responses proposed, and in some cases implemented. The intensity of the panic can perhaps be attributed to the convergence of two factors. First, the introduction of new and dramatically different media of communication has always precipitated waves of social anxiety. The early movie industry was denounced in many quarters as subversive of morals, and Hollywood as Sodom and Gomorrah; film censorship exercised by national and local governments followed directly in the wake of film distribution to theaters. Like television, itself subject to rising pressures for censorship, the Internet seems especially subversive as it comes directly into the home and is thus readily available to children (who may be more technologically savvy than their parents). Its borderless character is further cause for panic. Second, Internet technology has coincided with heightened social and cultural tensions in many Western societies along ethnic, racial, and gender divisions. Anti-pornography campaigns have forged unusual alliances of moral majoritarian conservatives and militant feminists. Multicultural renegotiation of traditional hegemonies has encouraged demands for legal prohibitions against hate propaganda. At the same moment, the frontier atmosphere on the Internet seems to have channelled a great deal of pornographic and racist expression into the new medium, where the greatest freedom from censorship and regulation prevails. Once again, the age-old cry, "there ought to be a law" is sounded in the land, a cry that ironically comes more often than not from those who are otherwise vehement about free-market principles and keeping the state off the back of the society.

As is so often the case in such panics, the medium gets confused with the message. The Internet itself, and the panoply of new communications technologies in which it is embedded, becomes for some the focus of attack, rather than the uses or abuses to which the medium can be put. But the unusual nature of this new technology does make censorship a much more complex, difficult, perhaps even intractable, problem. Here again, we see one of the central paradoxes of this new technology, which simultaneously empowers its users and makes them vulnerabe to supervision and control.

The freedom of expression of a racist, an anti-Semite, a pedophile, or a misogynist rape-fantasist can be a direct threat, or at least a cause of hurt and anxiety, to racial minorities, Jews, children, women. This is, of course, just as true of the Internet as of other media of expression, such as print or video. The difference with the Internet is that other media are inherently more amenable to control and regulation, or even prohibition, by local governments. In the case of other media, production and distribution take place at specific points where laws can be enforced. Cyberspace transcends borders. A website might be put together in one location but, once on the Web, it moves like quicksilver. A rather trivial example: certain countries, like Canada and France, have banned publication of political poll results for a prescribed period of time preceding a national election. National elections were held in both these countries in 1997, and in both election websites were set up that, among other things, communicated poll results. When the cut-off time arrived that effectively prevented newspapers and radio and TV stations from reporting polls, some of these websites simply jumped to so-called mirror sites located in other countries, thereby removing themselves from national jurisdiction, even though they remained just as accessible to nationals as they had been before jumping.[61] So how can national states censor Internet sites that can elude their jurisdiction even as they target the national citizenry with their messages or images? Can the freedom of the messengers be limited so as to minimize the vulnerability of those threatened by the messages?

There is no doubt that public opinion is clamoring for controls over the Net. A Canadian survey showed strong demand for censorship, with women, especially mothers of young children, in the forefront. Sixty-six percent of Canadian adults approved government regulation. The pollster suggested that technological difficulties in censoring the Web were no deterrent to these respondents: "There's a moral imperative at play. People might know there are technical obstacles but they want somebody to keep trying anyway."[62] With public opinion aroused, politicians are not far behind. The initial response of the U.S. government was in line with the "there ought to be a law" nostrum. The Clinton administration passed the Communications Decency Act, which sought to shield children from indecent material on-line, by making it a crime punishable by up to two years in prison and $250,000 in fines to publish indecent material on the Internet in a manner available to those under eighteen years old. This was immediately challenged by civil libertarians and parts were quickly shot down by the Supreme Court as unconstitutional. This has not deterred state legislatures from trying to pass their own laws, nor Congress from introducing modified versions of the failed act.[63] However, attention has now shifted to a more ingenious version of Net self-censorship. The Platform for Internet Content Selection, or PICS, is adapted to large-scale computer servers, works with Microsoft's Web browser, and looks for electronic tags fixed to specific sites which are blocked when users undertake a specific search. The user sees only the matches, and is unaware of sites blocked. Companies like CyberPatrol and NetNanny develop lists of what is acceptable, using a combination of automated searches for keywords and their own value judgment. Vice President Al Gore has lauded this development and urged parents and interested citizens to add a populist note to the filter process by nominating their own finds of objectionable material for the proscribed site lists.[64] Institutions such as libraries and schools that provide extensive computer facilities have brought in their own filters or have even been threatened with loss of federal government funding if they fail to follow suit.[65] Some civil libertarians have begun to wonder if in their successful fight against the Communications Decency Act, they have not actually outsmarted themselves. Decentralized, opaque, non-governmental filtering might turn out to be much worse than the old bogy of state censorship, as Harvard law professor Lawrence Lessig argues. PICS can be imposed by anybody in the distribution chain. Thus a filter can be placed on a person's computer, or at the level of a company, an Internet service provider, or even a nation, without the knowledge of the end user, making it easier for centralized censors. "Taken together, filtering software and PICS lead to a hard-wired architecture of blocking that is antagonistic to the original free-wheeling and speech-enhancing values of the Internet."[66]

As experience with PICS and the practices of CyberPatrol and NetNanny and other such services has begun to accumulate, criticism has risen of the standards employed by these private censors. For instance, gay and lesbian groups have found that their sites are routinely excluded, whether on the basis of homophobic assumptions or simply on the basis of word searches that turn up negative flags on words such as "sex" is not clear. In some cases, ideological judgments are fairly blatant: NOW, the National Organization of Women, had a site blocked because CyberPatrol declared that "It's well known their bias is lesbian [!]." In some cases, censorship may simply be the inadvertent result of the limitations of word searches. A soccer club that used the term "boys 12 and under" was blocked as a potential pedophile site.[67] Yet there is a real question of accountability; to whom, in such a decentralized and privatized system, does one effectively complain? This question is especially complicated when the filters are developed with the participation of concerned citizens.

It is ironic that the decentered, diffuse world of the Internet may have developed a diffuse, decentered method of self-censorship that will prove very difficult to confront, much less comprehend. Old-fashioned, centralized state censorship in liberal democracies was at least fairly traceable.

FROM TAYLORISM TO TRANSPARENCY: WATCHED WORKERS

The paradox of increased empowerment and vulnerability is especially acute with regard to the extension of new information technologies into the workplace. Taylorism, or scientific management, with its time and motion studies of worker efficiency, represented a leading panoptic ideology in the Fordist, or assembly line, phase of industrial capitalism.[68] The computerization of the workplace, along with other new technologies of institutional surveillance such as smart IDs and electronic tags, might seem to represent a simple extension of management's power over workers, and so it has been described by some observers and critics.[69] It has also been described as the killer of jobs and the creator of permanent mass unemployment and underemployment.[70] This second issue raises another set outside the scope of this book. However, for employed workers, the computerized workplace may be a more complex and ambiguous situation than the notion of electronically extended Taylorism would suggest. For many workers, a networked computer represents empowerment in daily tasks. If it were no more than a matter of a quantitative increase in the speed with which transactions could be completed, computerization would mean merely a speed-up of production, and thus enhanced Taylorism. This may indeed be the case for many workers who find themselves obliged to run at the speed of the computer network, instead of the assembly line. But in many cases, computerization means a certain devolution of responsibility downward from supervisory management to front-line or street-level workers.

To take one instance, the introduction of on-board computers linked to extensive data bases in police cars has coincided with the emergence of "community policing" as a popular new model which, among other things, allows street-level officers to take more decisions on the spot. A wealth of data may be immediately available to a police officer in a patrol car based on a piece of information as simple as a vehicle licence number. The identity, residence, occupation, Social Security number, criminal record if any, and perhaps even financial records, of the registered vehicle owner may be called up by a few key strokes. At the same time, incident reports can be filed without a return to the police station. These developments have a double effect. Undeniably they blur hierarchy and decenter traditional supervision structures. According to Richard Ericson and Kevin Haggerty, "Communication technology permits the dispersal of policing structures and tasks into myriad microcenters of knowledge and power."[71] Yet according to the same authors, "every keystroke on the keyboard also 'types' the police officer in terms of the quality and quantity of his or her knowledge production and thereby disciplines the officer as a useful worker, without the need for direct supervisory intervention . . . the computer terminal in the patrol car is a time-and-motion study that never ends."[72] In terms of traditional notions of power and authority, this double result might seem deeply contradictory. In light of new technologies and the accompanying transformations of the communications and authority structures, there is no contradiction. Workers are more closely monitored than ever before, but the dispersal of information simultaneously reorganizes the structure of supervision both vertically and horizontally. Computers in a sense allow individual workers to supervise themselves.

Another dramatic effect of computerization is the physical dispersal of work sites. In fully computerized organizations, especially those that do not physically produce goods, there is no longer the same requirement for a centralized location. Hence, "telecommuting" and the peripheral home office. At one level this permits workers greater choice and convenience in where they do their work, and reduced transportation costs and commuting time. At another level, it is simply a reflection of the extended surveillance capacities of the organization that can now reach into workers' homes and precisely record their hours of work and their productivity. As befits the high-tech industry's place at the cutting edge, Silicon Valley has taken this process a step further:

Global telecommuting, through which [U.S.] technology companies have created a whole new realm of international trade by exporting their work and hiring programmers overseas to do it. Having already scooped up any American programmers they could by offering them the chance to ride the Internet to work from their homes in Jackson Hole, Wyo., or Boulder, Colo., the corporations are now reaching out to places like South Africa and the Philippines. So increasingly, the world's commerce involves not just tankers filled with Brent crude or container ships laden with VCRs, but cables buzzing with computer programming code, product designs and engineering diagrams and formulas.[73]

Nevertheless, the information technology industry has asked the U.S. government for changes in immigration regulations to permit more programmers to emigrate to the United States. Virtual immigration is not apparently good enough, and old-fashioned real immigration is required when a shortage in certain skills is felt. This points to a limit in the telecommuting concept. The people used as global teleworkers are basically second-stringers, doing jobs like debugging programs, cleaning up details. For innovation, a certain human concentration is required to produce the synergy needed for creativity. Hence, the nodes in the global networks around places such as Silicon Valley.

Telecommuting even within regions has proven to be less effective at the managerial, research, and development levels than at the lower ends of the work scale. The jobs most successfully decentralized into individual workers' homes turn out to be the electronic equivalents of sweatshop work, like people who handle and route telephone orders for pizza delivery services. From management's point of view, such offloaded jobs transfer office maintenance costs to the workers, evade occupational health and safety obligations, and by isolating workers, discourage solidarity and union organization. These are the kind of jobs where remote surveillance can be effectively exercised while conceding the least decision-making powers to the employees. But this kind of supercharged Taylorism will not work for most organizations as a whole and certainly not for the middle and upper job ranges, where people will have the freedom to work in more flexible situations and to be much more mobile with their work, but who will still tend to cluster in physical proximity with one another.

The cyberserfs toiling in their own homes and apartments on a commission basis are not generally plugged into a two-way communication system. Instead, they are more likely manning systems not yet fully automated, but heading in that direction. E-mail as a communication tool within management itself exhibits a rather different character. For one thing, e-mail eliminates from communication the hierarchical cues that infect face-to-face communication. Women need not be silenced by domineering male voices, discussion can be more color-blind, etc. Studies of the impact of e-mail communication in transnational corporations suggests a slight flattening of hierarchical order, a certain limited democratization. Unfortunately, there is a downside to this: people also report higher degrees of insecurity and uncertainty when faced with the dilemmas of operating within what are, at the end of the day, hierarchical organizations with fewer clear guidelines or protocols of behavior. Democratization has a volatile side as well. Unable to effect genteel putdowns by the body language of status and privilege, or unable to catch the cues that would signal retreat and submission, participants sometimes resort to verbal violence: the phenomenon of "flaming" one's opponents by nasty verbal assaults.[74]

It is very difficult to generalize about the impact of the new information technologies on work. David Lyon suggests that the term "disorganized surveillance" might be an appropriate characterization.[75] New technologies are transforming the organizations and work, but the present is a period of transition, the outcome of which is very cloudy. But the central paradox is clear enough. Empowerment and increased vulnerability are intimately linked in the process of decentered surveillance.

NOTES TO CHAPTER 4

1. Robert Uhlig, "Spy Camera Keeps a Private Eye on Au Pairs," *Daily Telegraph*, 16 December 1997; Gary Strauss, "Nanny Cams Ease Parental Angst," *USA Today*, 26 February 1998.

2. A good critical discussion of video cameras can be found in Peter J. Schuurman, *Spying, Peeping and Watching Over: The Beguiling Eyes of Video Surveillance* (Queen's University, MA Sociology Dept. 1995).

3. David M. Halbfinger, "Spread of Surveillance Cameras Raises Prospect of Prying Eyes," *New York Times*, 22 February 1998.

4. Felicia R. Lee, "Cameras Drive Drug Dealers From Greenwich Village Park," *New York Times,* 3 January 1998.

5. Michael Cooper, "Public TV Surveillance Draws Mixed Reactions," *New York Times*, 5 February 1997.

6. Evelyn Nieveseast, "Welcoming 'Big Brother' Watchfully: Public TV Surveillance Draws Mixed Reactions," *New York Times*, 5 February 1997.

7. "In a Small Town, Cameras Keep Watch," *New York Times*, 7 December 1997.

8. Paul Brown, "Demand for Closed Circuit TV Triggers Fear of Crime," *The Guardian*, 9 January 1998.

9. Teresa Riordan, "Engineer Invents Computerized Surveillance System," *New York Times*, 13 October 1997.

10. Saul Hansell, "Use of Recognition Technology Grows in Everyday Transactions," *New York Times*, 20 August 1997; Michael Stutz, "Saving Face With Person Spotter," *Wired News* [on-line], 19 February 1998.

11. A test of an iris-scanning lens at ATMs was announced in the United Kingdom in late 1997. The technology "can recognise an individual's eye-print—the unique pattern found on the iris, the coloured ring of tissue surrounding the pupil. Each person has a different pattern of filaments, pits and striations in the iris, making it as distinctive as a fingerprint." An authorized user has his or her pattern recorded, then reduced to a digital code. "Then, each time they use their card, they will have to look into a camera from a distance of about one foot. The iris scan will be extracted from the image, and compared with the stored code held in a central data base to confirm the individual's identity." Nigel Hawkes, "Machines Will Pay up in Blink of an Eye," *The Times* (London), 2 December 1997.

12. David Banisar, "Big Brother Goes High-Tech," *Covert Action Quarterly* 56 (1996).

13. Steve Wright, *An Appraisal of Technologies for Political Control* (Luxembourg: European Parliament, Directorate General for Research, 1998), 4.1.

14. Fox Butterfield, "Devices May Let Police Spot People on the Street Hiding Guns," *New York Times*, 7 April 1997.

15. Jeffrey T. Richelson, "Scientists in Black," *Scientific American* (February 1998) 48–55.

16. Alexander Wooley, "Precision Farming" *The Globe & Mail* [Toronto], 15 March 1997.

17. Warren L. Strutzman and Carl B. Dietrich, Jr., " Moving Beyond Wireless Voice Systems," *Scientific American* (April 1998), 92–3.

18. Michael Learmonth, "Sky Spy," *Metro*, April 16–22.

19. Jim Wolf, "Colorado Spy-quality Satellite Ready to Sell Images," *Reuters*, 25 December 1998.

20. Gerald Steinberg, "Dual Use Aspects of Commercial High-resolution Imaging Satellites," *Mideast Security and Policy Studies*, 37 (February 1998).

21. Paul Nuki, "Snoopers to Get Eye in the Sky," *Sunday Times*, 16 February 1997.

22. Steve Connor, "Menagerie of Cyberbeasts Begins March Out of the Laboratory," *The Times* [London], 13 April 1997.

23. Margaret Webb Pressler, "Clandestine Recorders Get the Buzz," *Los Angeles Times*, 23 January 1998.

24. Jeffrey T. Richelson and Desmond Ball, *The Ties That Bind: Intelligence Coopera-*

tion Between the UKUSA Countries (Boston: Allen & Unwin, 1985); James Bamford, *The Puzzle Palace: Inside the National Security Agency, America's Most Secret Intelligence Organization* (N.Y.: Penguin Books, 1983).

25. Mike Frost, an ex-employee of the Canadian agency, the CSE, has written a controversial exposé: Frost, *Spyworld: Inside the Canadian and American Intelligence Establishments* (Toronto: Doubleday, 1994).

26. Nicky Hager, *Secret Power: New Zealand's Role in the International Spy Network* (Nelson, New Zealand: Craig Potton Publishing, 1996), 29.

27. Margie Wylie, "Who's Your PC Talking To?," *Perspectives*, 11 February 1998.

28. John V. Evans, "New Satellites for Personal Communications," *Scientific American* (April 1998), 70–77.

29. Alison Mitchell, "Ohio Congressman Threatens Suit Over Intercepted Conference Call," *New York Times*, 13 November 1997.

30. John Markoff, "High-Tech Eavesdropping Raises New Questions on Personal Privacy," *New York Times*, 13 October 1997.

31. Peter Wayner, "Technology That Tracks Cell Phones Draws Fire," *New York Times*, 23 February 1998; Chris Oakes, " 'E911' Turns Cell Phones Into Tracking Devices," *Wired News*, 6 January 1998.

32. David Lyon, *The Electronic Eye: the Rise of Surveillance Society* (Minneapolis: University of Minnesota Press, 1994), 102–7.

33. Richard Ford, "Tagging for 6,000 Freed Prisoners," *The Times* [London], 17 February 1998.

34. Richard Cole, "FBI Says Hacker Took 100,000 Credit Card Numbers," *New York Times*, 23 May 1997.

35. Michael White, "Technology That Guides Missiles Is Used to Zero In on Card Thieves," *New York Times*, 24 September 1997.

36. Laurie J. Flynn, "New Products Expand Recognition-Technology Market," *New York Times*, 8 February 1998.

37. Ben Elgin, "Web-accessible records jeopardize InternetUser," *ZD Internet Magazine*, 2 September 1997; Margot Williams & Robert O"Harrow, Jr., "On-line Searches Fill in May Holes," *Washington Post*, 8 March 1998; Blaine Harden, "Paranoids Find a Reason to Be Paranoid," *Washington Post*, 6 August 1997.

38. Valerie Elliott, "ID Smartcards Back on Agenda, Says Minister: Whitehall's Planned Electronic Revolution Will Mean 'Joined-up Government,'" *The Times* (London). 11 February 1998.

39. See Chapter Seven.

40. Ronald J. Deibert, *Parchment, Printing, and Hypermedia: Communications in World Order Transformation* (N.Y.: Columbia University Press, 1997), 47–110.

41. Charles Pappas, "To Surf and Protect," *Yahoo Internet Life* (December 1997).

42. "Tech Firms: Don't Worry, We'll Guard Your Privacy," *Reuters*, 8 December 1997.

43. Katharine Q. Seelye, "Companies Agree to Protect Personal Data," *New York Times*, 18 December 1997.

44. "FTC to Survey Web Privacy Policies," *Wired News*, 2 March 1998.

45. John Markoff, "Pact to Test Controls on Data," *New York Times*, 18 December 1997.

46. Robert O'Harrow, Jr., "Picking up on cookie crumbs," *Washington Post*, 9 March 1998.

47. "Net could revolutionize phone service: New phone technology could be "unstoppable"' *USA Today*, 10 February 1998.

48. Ashley Dunn, "The Fall and Rise of Privacy," *New York Times*, 24 September 1997.

49. Amitai Etzioni, "Some Privacy, Please, for e-mail," *The New York Times*, 23 November 1997.

50. See Chapter Six.

51. Jon Dillon, "Are the Feds sniffing your re-mail?", *Covert Action Quarterly* (June 1996).

52. See Chapter One.

53. Wayne Madsen, "Crypto AG: the NSA's Trojan Horse?", *Covert Action Quarterly* 63 (inter 1998).

54. Ashley Dunn, "Of Keys, Decoders and Personal Privacy," *New York Times*, 1 October 1997.

55. Peter Wayner, "British Document Outlines Early Encryption Discovery," *New York Times*, 24 December 1997.

56. "Team of Computer Enthusiasts Cracks Government-Endorsed DES Algorithm in Less Than Half the Time of Previous Challenge," *PRNewswire*, 26 February 1998.

57. Greg Miller, "Firms Agree on Digital Anti-Piracy Technology," *Los Angeles Times*, 19 February 1998.

58. Jeri Clausing, "Support for Encryption Is Less Than U.S. Claims, Study Says," *New York Times*, 9 February 1998.

59. A summary of findings was been released in late 1997: The President's Commission on Critical Infrastructure Protection, *Critical Foundations: Thinking Differently*. See Peter Wayner, "U.S. Commission finds that nation is vulnerable to cyber-terrorism," *New York Times*, 23 October 1997; and Chris Oakes, "A New Crypto Furor," *Wired News* 7 November 1997.

60. See Chapter Six.

61. Andy Riga, "Web sites move south to dodge election law," *Montreal Gazette*, 30 May 1997.

62. Chris Cobb, "Rein in the Net, Canadians Say," *Montreal Gazette*, 22 December 1997.

63. Jeri Clausing, "States Keep Up Efforts on Internet Restrictions," *New York Times*, 19 February 1998.

64. Jeri Clausing,"Gore Announces Efforts to Patrol Internet," *New York Times*, 3 December 1997.

65. Pamela Mendels, "Plan Linking Internet Subsidy to Filters Finds Critics," *New York Times* 24 January 1998.

66. Carl S. Kaplan, "Is a Better CDA Preferable To Opaque Censorship?," *New York Times*, 30 October 1997.

67. Carl S. Kaplan, "Filtering Companies Assailed for Blocking 'Unpopular' Voices," *New York Times*, 11 December 1997; Matt Richtel, "Filters Use Different Approaches And Get Different Results," *New York Times*, 31 January 1998.

68. See Chapter Two.

69. Heather Menzies, *Whose Brave New World? The Information Highway and the New Economy* (Toronto: between The Lines, 1996), 125–28.

70. David F. Noble, *Progress Without People: New Technology, Unemployment, and the Message of Resistance* (Toronto: Between The Lines, 1995).

71. Richard V. Ericson and Kevin D. Haggerty, *Policing the Risk Society* (Toronto: University of Toronto Press, 1997), 435.

72. Ibid., 432.

73. Allen R. Myerson, "Virtual Migrants: Need Programmers? Surf Abroad," *New York Times* 18 January 1998.

74. Lee Sproull and Sara Kiesler, "Computers, Networks and Work," *Scientific American* (September 1991).

75. Lyon, *The Electronic Eye*, 119–135.

5—Dark Towers:
Data Bases and Alienation

We have reviewed the new technologies of surveillance. Now we turn to the *uses* to which information gathered by surveillance can be put. The new information technologies have facilitated the gathering of information, and the same technologies facilitate the storage, retrieval, and processing of information. These converge in data bases, the concentration of systematically organized information in relatively secure holdings, owned and operated by governments, corporations, or other organizations for specific institutional purposes. Data bases are not like libraries, in which books, magazines, newspapers, etc. are collected for whatever use readers may choose to make of them. Data bases are collections of information acquired and organized for very directed purposes. Indeed, the raw information itself is gathered in line with a specific design: the data are chosen to answer certain questions, and the structure of data bases—their classifications, their ordering, the signals or switches for retrieval—reflects this design.

In their structure and purposes, data bases parallel the files or dossiers of intelligence agencies or security police. They are just as purposefully acquired and organized, and they are designed to be operational. They are cumulative and expansionary. And they have something else in common: *they feed on themselves*. The bigger and more detailed the data base or dossier, the greater the capacity to extract yet more useful information. Data bases are like intelligence investigations. The more information is collected, the more leads are opened up pointing to yet more sources. In both cases, the new information technologies accelerate all the processes involved. Collection of data, its storage and its retrieval can all be to varying degrees automated, and thus enormously speeded up.

Data bases diverge from intelligence dossiers in at least three significant ways. First, security and intelligence information is mainly, although not exclusively, composed of secret information that is purposefully withheld or concealed by others. Data bases rarely contain information that has to be collected by covert means, although that kind of information may make up a part of certain kinds of data bases (criminal records or taxation data, for instance). For the most part, however, data bases—especially those in the private sector—are composed of information that is freely or consensually acquired. This is an important difference. The uses made of consensually acquired information in data bases are, however, very imperfectly connected to the original grounds for consent—an important distinction to which I shall return later.

A second distinction between data bases and intelligence dossiers is that the latter, having been acquired in secrecy and by covert collection, tend to be jealously guarded and are shared only in carefully calculated secret exchanges or information barters with other agencies engaged in the same kind of business. Data base operators, on the other hand, tend to regard their data as a commodity that can and should be sold. Impediments to marketing data are usually externally imposed: laws and government regulations; self-regulating industrial codes of conduct; even the pressures of competition in certain markets. Government agencies often find themselves restricted by law and practice in the uses to which they can put their exclusive data, although this too is opening up rapidly as governments are encouraged to market their services on cost-recovery criteria, or privatize them on a for-profit basis. Generally, the dynamic is toward commodification and marketing of data. So great is this push that data bases have generated an entire new stratum of information brokers, and indeed data base operators increasingly act as information brokers themselves.

The third difference, closely related to the second, is that security and intelligence dossiers are highly centralized in location and in the structure of hierarchical control over the data. Not surprisingly, they have acted historically as buttresses of strong centralized states. Data bases, on the other hand, tend to be horizontally dispersed and decentralized. Their rise has coincided with the decentering of the state, a relative decline in state power, and the dominance of markets over politics.

I have stressed the contrasts between intelligence dossiers and data bases for a particular reason. Both contain personal information on citizens and this information is collected in both cases with a view to its potential uses. Both collection processes are premised on the assumption that such information has value, that it constitutes a form of *power*. But power is interpreted rather differently through the prism of these two different processes of information collection and organization. The centralized, secret model has been in part displaced by the newer decentralized, commodified model, although the two continue to run in parallel, utilizing the same information technologies in somewhat differing ways. However, there are important similarities. Whether public or private, government or corporate, data bases generally contain data that is machine-readable and network-linked. The data is usually designed for one or both of two broad objectives: (1) risk evaluation and exclusion, and (2) consumer identification and inclusion. Data bases provide an informational structure that is inferential and predictive. That is why they are so useful to governments and corporations. They can tell them who to exclude as risks and who to target as customers or clients.

FROM SURVEILLANCE TO DATAVEILLANCE

The term dataveillance has been coined to "describe the surveillance practices that the massive collection and storage of vast quantities of personal data have facilitated."[1] The key to how a decentralized, dispersed, and apparently disorganized system of data bases can be managed and coordinated is digitization. Digital is the universal language that permits data bases to "talk" to one another. To shift metaphors, digital is a universal currency that permits data flow. Data bases are organized on particular principles, but data from one data base can easily be read and incorporated into another data base, hence the facile commodification of data. One of the crucial elements in the transformation of data into a commodity is the practice of data-matching or data-linkage, whereby separately collected and separately organized pieces of data are matched or linked to produce new and valuable information. Examples might be a life insurance company matching its policy-holder records with medical data and learning that certain categories constitute an increased cancer risk, requiring higher premiums. Or a marketing firm matching consumer data on the audience for a specialized television channel with the product line of one of its client companies and discovering a new advertising spot for its client. Data-linkage opens up the field for data brokers and allows for data-mining, in which data from multiple data bases is purposefully scanned and exploited for profit. For instance, data on births might be utilized by companies selling baby products in conjunction with data bases providing socioeconomic data on consumers to produce a specific set of marketing targets. All these dataveillance practices point to an important observation: *data bases, despite their dispersed and decentralized structure, form a more or less unified functional system.*

Oscar Gandy identifies eleven different categories of personal information that now reside routinely in public and private data banks in machine-readable, network-linked data files. These categories are:

(1) *personal information for identification and qualification*
includes birth certificate, driver's licence, passport, voter registration, automobile registration, school records, marriage certification

(2) *financial information*
includes bank records, savings passbooks, ATM cards, credit cards, [debit cards, cash cards, online banking files], credit reports/files, tax returns, stock/brokerage accounts, traveller's checks

(3) *insurance information*
includes insurance for health, automobile, home, business, general and specific liability, group and individual policies

(4) *social services information*
includes social security, health care, employment benefits, unemployment benefits, disability, pensions, food stamps and other government assistance, veterans' benefits, senior citizens' benefits/subsidies

(5) *utility services information*
> includes telephone, electricity, gas, cable television, [Internet service], sanitation, heating, garbage, security, delivery

(6) *real estate information*
> involved with purchase, sale, rental, lease

(7) *entertainment/leisure information*
> includes travel itineraries, recreational profiles, automobiles and other rentals/leases, lodging reservations, airplane reservations, ship reservations, train reservations, entertainment tickets/ reservations, newspaper and periodical subscriptions, television/cable rating

(8) *consumer information*
> includes merchant credit cards, other accounts, layaway, leases and rentals, purchases, purchase inquiries, subscriber lists, clothing and shoe sizes

(9) *employment information*
> includes application, medical examination, references, performance assessments, employment history, employment agency applications

(10) *educational information*
> includes school applications, academic records, references, extracurricular activities/memberships, awards and sanctions, rankings

(11) *legal information*
> includes court records, lawyer's records, newspaper reports, index and abstract services[2]

How is all this kind of data gathered? Much of it is obtained from information provided in answer to forms, surveys, and questionnaires. Sometimes this information is compulsory. In the case of tax records, you might go to jail if you refuse to provide the required information. Sometimes the information is as good as compulsory—for instance, questions asked in a job application: if you refuse to answer, you will simply be excluded from the benefit of the job. Sometimes the information is voluntary, as in the case of the lifestyle and consumer-preference questionnaires attached to product warranty and registration cards, or on registration procedures for entry to websites. In many cases, whether voluntary or compulsory, the information gathered may appear to be for a particular purpose, but there is no guarantee that it will not be put to very different uses, often by parties other than the one that collected the information in the first instance. In an increasing number of cases, the person disclosing his or her personal information does not know that any such transfer is taking place, let alone to what end uses the information may be put. This is most often the case with data transferred as a result of transaction records, such as credit card purchases. The simple act of offering a credit card for scanning or swiping might occasion an instantaneous but invisible flow of data backward to the credit card company's data bases or forward to the merchant's consumer data bases. From thence, data could continue to flow in various directions. Note that with each new data match, there may be new value added, but that none of this additional value ever comes back, directly at least, to the individual whose information is being used. Though personal, the information has no rental value to its original owner. It is valuable, however, to the various actors who have appropriated this information for their own purposes.

Data bases can target categories of people and/or individuals. Government data bases tend to be highly personalized. Taxation data, for instance, is precisely individualized by a series of transaction records that locate and describe a specific individual's personal financial profile through identifier numbers, such as Social Security, that are attached to each transaction. An individual taxpayer reports his or her income and earnings, but that report can be checked by the state against data it holds quite independently of the taxpayer, and verified or flagged for a detailed audit and investigation. However personalized, this data is also used to fit the individual into a set of broad subcategories of the abstract concept "taxpayer." Data on income level will sort individual taxpayers into tax brackets that will be assessed differentially under progressive income tax schemes. Does the individual taxpayer fit into one or more of the categories that permit specific exemptions or rebates? And so on. In an important sense, the personalization of the data is required only to make the categorization precise. The state is really not interested in Taxpayer X, as such, but in where Taxpayer X fits in its abstract schema of taxpayer categories; to do this, however, the state must "know" Taxpayer X and his or her financial affairs in rather intimate detail.

In some cases, where for instance certain taxpayers make themselves notorious by their behavior or embody a profile suggests evasion of the rules, state investigations may assume a personalized quality. Mafia figures who have managed to avoid prosecution for their operations have sometimes been caught by tax-evasion charges. Occasionally, those who have made themselves obnoxious to the ruling politicians find themselves at the receiving end of an investigation of their tax affairs. When this kind of thing happens, the targets will complain about being victimized by political or personal vendettas, and public opinion may or may not sympathize with them depending on the circumstances. Too much personalization in the state's focus sets off alarm signals that all is not impartial in the administration of public affairs. It is supposed to be a characteristic of the modern bureaucratic state that does not target individual citizens but rather treats its citizens evenhandedly based on the broad, depersonalized categories of administrative rule. The paradox is that to do this job evenhandedly, the state requires highly detailed information so as to categorize people efficiently. To this end, new information technologies produce ever more detailed data bases of personal information. Limitations on their use and controls over their possible abuse have thus been on the policy agendas of liberal democracies for some time, usually in the form of data protection laws and privacy commissions. But states have a clear interest in acquiring more and more data and in matching and linking the data they have acquired from various sources and housed within their own various data bases. Data protection as a specialized function of government is thus in constant tension with the inherent drive for unimpeded collection and use of data for the state's multiple purposes — and those assigned to protect data are in an immeasurably weaker position than the bureaucrats seeking out and using data.[3]

To make prospects for control of government data bases even dimmer, governments have increasingly been developing interfaces with the private sector that involve data transfers. Ericson and Haggerty, for instance, conclude from their study of policing that the speeded-up flow of information to police data bases, facilitated by the introduction of new information technologies, has transformed the police from one of the more secretive of government services into brokers of information to institutions such as insurance companies and health and welfare organizations. The common interest is risk avoidance.[4]

To the public and private sectors, risk avoidance represents rational economic behavior. To individuals adversely affected by the use of such data, the personal consequences can range from inconvenience to disaster. High automobile insurance rates may be annoying to affluent drivers, but seriously damaging to poorer drivers who depend on the use of their cars for their livelihood. What of cases where misinformation gets into the data bases, unfairly penalizing individuals? Large bureaucratic organizations tend to be oblivious to individual complainants, and resistant to allowing information in their data bases to be reviewed by outsiders—even when the "outsiders" are the individuals affected. Take the case of a California man, Bronti Kelly, who in 1990 lost his job as a department store salesman and has subsequently been turned down for dozens of retail sales jobs. When he has got a job, he has been typically fired within a couple of days. The reason? Kelly had his identification stolen in 1990 by a man who was later arrested for shoplifting. An arrest report under his name wound up in public court files. All Kelly's prospective employers were checking with a data base used by retail chains that taps court records. Although Kelly has received a "Certificate of Clearance" from the Los Angeles Police Department, that information is not included in the searchable on-line data base of court records, and the false report of his arrest stays in the retail chains' employment data base. So Kelly, who has had to declare bankruptcy, can't get a job in his profession. "It feels like I'm in the Twilight Zone," says Kelly. "I wish I could stop people getting into this record when they're looking me up, but there's nothing I can do. It's disgusting."[5]

LITTLE BROTHERS
CROWD OUT BIG BROTHER

Data-protection laws and watchdog agencies are much more likely to focus on the public than the private sectors. But not only is the public sector blurring into the private sector, in the United States, private-sector data bases are overshadowing the state in terms of their scope and reach into the day-to-day lives of citizens. With the kind of in-depth surveillance technology now available and with the scope for horizontal data-linkage, private information brokers are becoming very big business. Take Geographic Information Systems, or GIS, a

> cutting-edge technology putting detailed maps and high resolution aerial photographs into computerized form . . . This technology is proving an astonishingly powerful and lucrative commercial tool to crunch information from public records and private sector data banks and to spit out house-by-house information that can include everything from the tax assessment and the occupant's driver's license photograph, to details of consumer behavior. . . . GIS started as a way to map land, sea and sky across space and time. It has had enormously beneficial social uses, from pinpointing the origin of Legionnaire's disease to helping South Florida communities coordinate emergency relief after Hurricane Andrew.

The commercialization of the technology places it in a rather different light. In one application, "businesses can feed car license numbers from a parking lot into a program and retrieve a customer's name, address, census tract information and demographic characterizations. . . . Another program transforms a telephone number into a detailed profile of each prospective customer who calls an 800 number." The electronic monitoring of public spaces for safety and traffic planning can be used by GIS to track individuals or vehicles. This information can be correlated to a wealth of other data culled from computerized public records. Increasingly, cash-strapped government agencies are selling packaged public information to businesses or entering joint ventures to make the information more attractive to marketers. Only a decade ago, when the Federal Bureau of Investigation sought clearance to enter all national data bases, Congress said no. "Now the commercial market has done it for them." Government agencies like the FBI "just have to pay like anybody else."[6] GIS technology has spawned a booming industry that profiles people and households for data-based marketing, health care, insurance, real estate, and financial services. New mergers and partnerships have been formed with credit bureaus and data brokerages and data-miners to form giant data bases that are "continuously updated and parsed to yield an unprecedented level of detail on nearly everyone in the nation."

In this burgeoning world of data-base power, we might look at the Acxiom Corporation, hardly a household name, but described by the *New York Times* as a new force in the land:

> If information is like money, a company called the Acxiom Corporation is one of the merchant bankers of the age. . . . Its heart is behind the locked doors of what a guide calls "the production war rooms," low-ceilinged bunkers where six robots inside small linked silos match data tapes at 60 miles an hour, while 20 mainframe computers swallow 1.3 billion bytes of data a second. GIS is just part of the information infrastructure. Acxiom's revenue grew by almost 50 percent in fiscal 1997, to $402 million. Its top customers include data kings like the AT&T Corporation, Wal-Mart Stores, Citibank, a unit of Citicorp, IBM, the Allstate Corporation and ADP Automatic Data Processing, which handles half the payrolls in America. . . .[7]

Acxiom gathers and sorts information about 196 million Americans. It holds 350 trillion characters of consumer data in its data base. Twice a month, it receives every change of address filed with the U.S. Postal Service, so as never to be out of date. An Acxiom executive is quoted as saying that "the data has always been there, it's just that now, with the technology, you can access it . . . Today's it's almost unbounded, our ability to gather, sort and make sense of the vast quantities of data."[8]

The privacy implications of this concentration of data are multiple. One Ohio woman learned to her horror of one kind of problem when she received in the mail a handwritten twelve-page letter from a stranger who seemed to know all about her, "from her birthday to the names of her favorite magazines, from the fact that she was divorced to the kind of soap she used in the shower." These details were woven into a sexual fantasy that he threatened to put into action when he had the chance.

The letter writer was a convicted rapist and burglar serving time in a Texas state prison. He had learned [her] name, address and other personal information from one of the product questionnaires that she and millions of other consumers had received in the mail, innocently completed and sent back to post office boxes in Nebraska and New York on the promise of coupons and free samples. Their answers were delivered by the truckload to the Texas prison system, which was under contract to handle the surveys for the Metromail Corporation, a leading seller of direct marketing information. Hundreds of unpaid inmates, many of them sex offenders, entered the information on computer tapes for Metromail, which has a detailed data base on more than 90 percent of American households.[9]

The woman has launched a class-action suit against Metromail. Her story, as distasteful as it is, represents a low-end example of the privacy risks involved. More significant in the long run is the immense amount of detailed personal data on individuals that can be appropriated for private profit, with little or no accountability.

THE "DEATH OF PRIVACY"?

In *1984*, the subjects of Oceana had no private space free from the intrusive gaze of Big Brother. The state held a massive centralized data base that contained everything that needed to be known about each subject. States today have a far greater technological capacity for surveillance and data linkage and retrieval than Orwell ever imagined at their disposal, and some of the elements of the Big Brother state do exist. But it is the Little Brothers of the private sector who are collecting data about the lives of individuals—who know, for instance, what brand of soap an Ohio woman uses in her shower. What is more, the information that goes into these data bases is either given voluntarily (as in the case of the Ohio woman) or acquired silently and invisibly, without the subject's awareness. Big Brother commands information, as in tax reporting or census questions, and tends thereby to rouse resentment and even occasional resistance. Little Brothers, on the other hand, impact very little on people at the data-collection stage. There is no recognizable name to put to the dispersed but linked data bases of the private sector, while the state is personified in a leader and, in a democracy, is believed to be accountable to the public, at least in theory. Ironically, the one-way transparency sought by the Orwellian state has been realized much more effectively in the private than in the public sector, where transparency, to a degree at least, goes both ways. As one writer in the *New York Times* recently suggested: "Perhaps we were so intent on avoiding Orwell's totalitarian Big Brother that we did not notice the arrival of millions of tattletale busybodies."[10]

In an August 1997 *Time* magazine cover story on "The Death of Privacy,"[11] author Joshua Quittner suggests some ways to protect your privacy: using less credit, not filling out warranty cards, and disabling "cookies." However, he rejects the idea of government intervention and regulation. This is in keeping with the strong individualist and anti-statist thinking so prevalent in America. But conceptualizing privacy as a purely individual value or interest reinforces an atomistic individualism that sees the individual in inevitable conflict with the society, and defines privacy in negative terms, as "the right to be left alone." This, as Priscilla Regan argues, forms a weak basis for formulating public policy in this area.[12] She suggests rethinking privacy as a positive social or collective value. The democratic public realm benefits from the participation of free and equal individuals, whose autonomy is rooted in a secure sense of the self they can bring to the community of peers. Her argument makes a great deal of sense, but the individualistic view remains dominant. So long as it does, it is hard to see how the lone individual, even a small number of like-minded individuals taking individual actions, can really reverse the effects of dataveillance that is driven by so much money and corporate power.

Perhaps the concept of privacy is one "whose time has come and gone" in Calvin Gotlieb's words.[13] Gotlieb believes that "all protestations to the contrary, most people, when other interests are at stake, do not care enough about privacy to value it. . . . [T]he trade-offs where privacy has been sacrificed are now so common that, for all practical purposes, privacy no longer exists." Privacy, he adds, is not a serious political issue. And in this he is undoubtedly right. There are no votes in campaigning for privacy, and so few politicians undertake sustained campaigns on this issue. On the other hand, any number of politicians do champion extending surveillance, on the popular grounds of law and order and public security.

Perhaps the ultimate reason for the weakness of the movement against the encroachments of private data bases lies in the positive benefits most people perceive from handing over personal information to corporations and marketers. Our participation in the Panopticon is explored in the following chapter. For now, it is enough to recall that, as I earlier pointed out, data bases serve two broad objectives: risk evaluation (exclusionary), and consumer identification (inclusionary). Exclusion is perceived by many as something that happens to marginal people. The benefits of inclusion in the consumer economy are widely appreciated.

This appreciation deepens when the benefits appear to be targeted personally, as with new micro- or niche-marketing strategies that have been opened up by the new information technologies. Mass marketing—which still of course continues—is a very blunt instrument, a bit like the bombs dropped from planes in World War II: a visual or radar sighting of the target area was made from thousands of feet in the air, the doors were opened, the bombs dumped, and the crew hoped for the best. Today's niche marketing is more like the military's contemporary smart weapons: the targeting is precise and the delivery is monitored and guided all the way to impact. The key to the new smart marketing is information. Consumers are identified not as mass, undifferentiated markets, but as subgroups with very specific purchasing patterns and power. Data gathering on consumer preferences, if noticed at all by the targets, is seen as facilitating consumption. For instance, electronic checkouts at video rental shops speed up the process for customers. Few realize that information on each rental becomes part of a data profile of each customer's preferences in films.[14] For especially affluent consumers, micro marketing may become very personalized, indeed. Some grocery chains in the United States track weekly consumption patterns by preferred customers and may contact a customer personally to inquire into how they may be better served. The point is that if connections are seen between the disclosure of personal information and consumer data bases, they will likely be viewed in a positive rather than a negative light.

For those excluded, it would be hard to find anything positive in the exercise of surveillance. But even for those included, the benefits, while tangible enough, mask deeper issues that are very troubling. If privacy is conceptualized as the negative defense of the isolated stand-alone individual against society, its passing need not perhaps be mourned too deeply. But if we think of surveillance and privacy in social terms, as a complex of factors that shape the individual within society, the outlook is more worrisome.

WE ARE ALL OWEN LATTIMORES NOW

Readers may recall that in an earlier chapter[15] I described the role of internal security in liberal democracies, and the apparatus of screening for security risks. I recounted the case of the scholar Owen Lattimore who became a prime target for anti-Communist witch-hunters in the McCarthy era. Lattimore, who survived the ordeal, wrote memorably about how the security files had constructed a picture of a man *"who might have existed."*

Today, we are all, in a sense, Owen Lattimores. The private and public data bases that form the dark towers of cyberspace contain the shadow selves of almost every citizen and consumer. These data profiles, or shadow selves, in important ways overshadow our real selves.[16] "There really are ghosts," explains Don Goldhammer, a University of Chicago computer network administrator, "every one of us is followed around by an invisible profile that purports to be who we are."[17] People who have protested bad credit ratings, for instance, have found that even simple cases of mistaken identity have been almost impossible to rectify. Just as the guardians of state security always argued that doubt must be resolved in favor of the state, the powerful motive of risk aversion on the part of capital means that doubt is resolved in favor of the corporation. Corporations do not care if mistakes are made, or injustices perpetrated against individuals (except in the rare cases where sufficient bad publicity is generated that their public image suffers), because it does not *pay* to be attentive to such possibilities. They are in the business of avoiding risks on behalf of their shareholders; data profiles indicate risk categories, and actions are taken to avoid anyone whose profile places them in the category. The result is a kind of social triage. The result is that some people are effectively excluded from full citizenship, not in the state, but in civil society.

Our cyberspace selves tend to overshadow our real selves for both good and bad reasons. Data bases mirror the real world, but imperfectly. And this imperfection is structural, inherent. Just as a perfect scientific/mathematical model of the material universe — one that established a one-to-one relationship with reality — would be an absurdity, a theory as vast and complex as the actual universe, so too data profiles are always simplifications of reality. The key points are: Who asks the questions? Who sets the parameters of the data search? For what purposes and what interests? The answer of course is that those with wealth and power get to shape the questions and thus the kind of simplifications that emerge. Corporate data bases, and the public data bases to which corporations buy privileged access, exist to answer corporate questions. The simplified, perhaps simplistic, data profiles are patterned to answer corporate needs. Real-world selves are inveterately messy, maddeningly complex, irritatingly inconsistent, full of contradictions — in a word, difficult. That is what it means to be human, after all, and why we so often throw up our hands in personal relationships, write poems and novels and plays, toil over biographies, and try vainly as social scientists to explain individual behavior through meta-theories. But our cyberspace shadow selves are not messy, not complex, not inconsistent, not contradictory: they are simple, easy constructs that can be quickly and cheaply drawn from the data base and cost-efficiently used by the customers who pay for them. These cartoons crowd out the messy reality because the world of economic transactions is structured in such a way that only certain kinds of information can be fed into it. If you don't fit the program, you will have to be cut down to size, or stretched, or whatever it takes. It's the Mad Hatter's Tea Party; if the dormouse can't be stuffed into the teapot, he will just have be excluded — a *risk*.

The new information technologies have promised a great deal, and have even opened up a new parallel universe — cyberspace. This parallel universe is exciting, but it can also be a threatening terrain, where dark towers of data brood on the horizon, haunted by shadow distortions of our selves that menace or ridicule us in our daily lives. It is an alienated world where the products of our own invention can come back to torment us.

NOTES TO CHAPTER 5

1. Colin J. Bennett, "The Public Surveillance of Personal Data: A Cross-national Analysis," in David Lyon & Elia Zureik, eds., *Computers, Surveillance, and Privacy* (Minneapolis: University of Minnesota Press, 1996), 237.

2. Oscar H. Gandy, Jr., *The Panoptic Sort: A Political Economy of Personal Information* (Boulder: Colo.: Westview Press, 1993), 63, and Gandy, "Coming to Terms With the Panoptic Sort," in Lyon & Zureik, *Computers*, 139. I have interpolated some additional elements within square brackets.

3. David H. Flaherty, *Protecting Privacy in Surveillance Societies: The Federal Republic of Germany, Sweden, France, Canada, and the United States* (Chapel Hill, N.C.: The University of North Carolina Press, 1989).

4. Richard V. Ericson & Kevin D. Haggerty, *Policing the Risk Society* (Toronto: University of Toronto Press, 1997).

5. Rajiv Chandrasekaran, "Doors Flung Open to Public Records," *Washington Post*, 8 March 1998.

6. Nina Bernstein, "Lives on File: Privacy Devalued in Information Economy," *New York Times*, 12 June 1997.

7. Bernstein, op. cit.

8. Robert O'Harrow, Jr., "Are Data Firms Getting too Personal?," *Washington Post*, 8 March 1998.

9. Bernstein, op. cit.

10. Peter H. Lewis, "Forget Big Brother," *New York Times*, 19 March 1998.

11. Joshua Quittner, "Invasion of Privacy," *Time*, 25 August 1997.

12. Priscilla Regan, *Legislating Privacy: Technology, Social Values, and Public Policy* (Chapel Hill: University of North Carolina Press, 1995).

13. Calvin C. Gotlieb, "Privacy: A Concept Whose Time Has Come and Gone," in Lyon & Zureik, *Computers*, 156–71.

14. Republican Supreme Court nominee Robert Bork learned about this to his dismay when undergoing Senate confirmation a few years ago: enemies got hold of the information that he had in the past rented pornographic films.

15. Chapter 1.

16. Mark Poster was one of the first to point out the existence and some of the significance of this shadow world: *The Mode of Information*, op. cit.

17. John Schwartz & Robert O'Harrow, Jr., "Databases Start to Fuel Consumer Ire," *Washington Post*, 10 March 1998.

6—The Participatory Panopticon

Santa Claus is a fairy tale taught to children. Like most such myths, it is supposed to be exemplary, to teach children to be good. It also embodies a crucial element of contemporary capitalist culture. Punishment means exclusion from the positive benefits of the consumer society. In Bentham's Panopticon, total surveillance and the implied threat of action against rule breakers trains the subjects to be docile, to internalize the rules within their own minds, thus preempting the actual exercise of direct sanctions. But the panoptic Santa adds a new dimension to the old idea, brings it up to date and improves it. The problem with the Bethamite, Taylorite, and Orwellian Panopticons was that they all cheated on the matter of consent and coercion. They claimed that coercion was replaced by active consent, but each of them depended fundamentally on coercion to maintain panoptic subjects in place: coercion was in the background only because it *was* the background. The contemporary Panopticon is strikingly different. It is a consumer Panopticon based on positive benefits where the worst sanction is exclusion. Bentham's prisoners would like nothing so much as to escape; the dissidents in Orwell's *1984* would be delighted to flee to somewhere better (but they can't, and there isn't). Our Panopticon is the source of goods.

BIG BROTHER LAID OFF: THE DECENTERED, CONSENSUAL PANOPTICON

The new Panopticon differs from the old in two significant ways: it is decentered and it is predominantly consensual. The first characteristic seems paradoxical. At the very core of the Benthamite idea was power rigorously centered, the architectural embodiment of godlike sovereign authority radiating out from the Inspector's command and control center. But this conceptualization is technologically obsolete at the end of the twentieth century. Bentham required this centralized architectural structure because he had no technology of surveillance other than the unassisted human eye. Elaborate artifice was required to trick the prisoners into believing in the Inspector's omniscience. The new information technologies offer the potential for real, rather than faked, omniscience, while at the same time displacing *The* Inspector with multiple inspectors who may act sometimes in concert and sometimes in competition with one another.

New technologies render individuals "visible," in ways that Bentham could not even conceive, but they are visible to multiple gazes coming from many different directions, looking for different things. Imagine a complex crisscrossing network of roving searchlights constantly lighting up individuals, who flare momentarily like fireflies, then disappear, only to be lit up again and again. It is an evanescent image that lacks the crude simplicity of Bentham's architecture, but it is closer to the complicated reality of today. Each time you make a purchase or engage in a financial transaction, each time you take any action that is recorded, somewhere (and fewer and fewer actions are not recorded, somewhere) you are briefly illuminated by the now ubiquitous, decentered Panopticon. That momentary transparency aggregated with all the other moments at which you are recorded through electronic data processing and data matching, yield a unified pattern. It is well known that new information technologies put many people out of work. What is less well known is that one of the first redundancies of the new era is The Inspector/Big Brother. There is less need for a central command centre, a single, focused Eye, when the same effect can be achieved by multiple, dispersed, even competitive eyes that in their totality add up to a system of surveillance more pervasive than that imagined by Orwell. The strength of this new Panopticon is that people tend to participate voluntarily because they see positive benefits from participation, and are less likely to perceive disadvantages or threats. They are not necessarily wrong to think this way, for the benefits are straightforward, real, and tangible. Disadvantages are less tangible, more indirect and more complex. They ought not, however, to be ignored.

The participatory Panopticon spreads its gaze seductively, yet insidiously. ATMs are a convenience, allowing one to do banking business at one's own expedience. Telephone and on-line banking offer even greater convenience, permitting financial transactions from one's home at any hour, any day. Credit, debit, and cash cards offer further extensions of this convenience, permitting purchases without the nuisance of worrying about cash at hand, and increasingly these cards allow purchases at a distance, by telephone or on-line that obviate having to travel to the place of business. Smart cards extend the convenience yet further, and they add a further benefit: security, as they can embed personal information that will prevent unauthorized use of the card.

Smart health cards can encode a large amount of personal health information. This presents distinct advantages. For instance, imagine if you were involved in a traffic accident, lying unconscious and bleeding on the ground. Emergency medical technicians arrive on the scene, locate your smart card, quickly scan it and read a variety of pertinent information: blood type, known allergies to medications, conditions that might cause complications, family physician, etc. Who could object to these positive benefits?

Surveillance for public safety is usually welcomed. The prevalence of video surveillance cameras in private spaces is increasingly being matched by video surveillance of public spaces. Criminal attacks are less likely in spaces under constant watch, and activity that degrades neighborhoods, such as drug dealing and prostitution, will tend to withdraw from areas of active surveillance. Intrusive surveillance by an oppressive government ("Big Brother is watching you!") rouses deep resentment, but what if the slogan appears rather as "Big Brother is watching out for you"?

These panoptic features all facilitate daily life, enhance security, and empower consumers. What if one's purchases are carefully recorded to construct a profile of consumption preferences for the use of various marketers? Not everyone will object to this if they see their needs and desires being better served as a result. Think of it as a Christmas wish list that enables Santa to serve you better. The consumer Panopticon rewards participation.

There is, alas, always a price to pay. Smart health cards offer benefits, but what if the same card yields information on medical insurance or lack thereof, credit worthiness or risk, or other information that might slam shut for-profit hospital emergency doors? What if it contains information on such matters as HIV status, mental illnes, or a history of drug abuse, or other information that could be devastating for the individual in various contexts? And, jumping ahead to the early twenty-first century, what happens when more and more of the human genome is mapped and genetic information on individuals becomes available?

Video surveillance makes people feel safer, and in conjunction with other sophisticated tracking technologies, offers greatly increased chances of finding missing persons, especially children. British writer Andrew O"Hagan in his book *The Missing* meditates on the terrible effect on the lives of parents, spouses, friends, who are left in fear and mystery when someone disappears. Yet he also acknowledges that disappearance often has to do with escaping:

> The missing problem can be complexly evil, and it can be complexly benign. It may in time be answered by a national system of watching which helps with the stamping out of all sorts of badness, but which also prevents people who want to lose themselves from doing so. This, perhaps, is the price to pay.[1]

There is always, it seems, a price to pay.

There is a still darker side that is invisible to the everyday user of these services. Those who use possess bank, credit, debit, and cash cards are empowered, but this depends on a disempowerment of others. The ability to extend credit to the creditworthy is made possible by the ability to identify and exclude the risky. The same Panopticon that issues inclusive benefits, punishes by exclusion. The same detailed surveillance that personalizes benefits, targets those to be excluded from benefits. Moreover, and here the seductiveness is truly insidious, consumers are being disciplined *by consumption itself* to obey the rules, to be "good" not because it is morally preferable to being "bad" but because there is no conceivable alternative to being good, other than being put outside the reach of benefits.

FROM MACHIAVELLI TO MICKEY MOUSE

In a brilliant metaphor a few years ago, criminologists Clifford Shearing and Philip Stenning used Disney World as the contemporary embodiment of panoptic power. Large numbers of people visit Disney World; there are often lengthy queues and long delays as families await entry to particular exhibits. Yet orderly, peaceful behavior is maintained in an apparently smooth and seamless manner, with no visible signs of coercion. This is made possible because of the shared desire of management and customers to facilitate consumption of Disney Productions:

> Within Disney World control is embedded, preventative, subtle, co-operative and apparently non-coercive and consensual. . . . Surveillance is pervasive but it is the antithesis of the blatant control of the Orwellian State: its source is not government and its vehicle is not Big Brother. The order of instrumental discipline is not the unitary order of a central State but diffuse and separate orders defined by private authorities responsible for the feudal-like domains of Disney World, condominium estates, commercial complexes and the like. Within contemporary discipline, control is as fine-grained as Orwell imagined but its features are very different. . . . [P]eople are today seduced to conform by the pleasures of consuming the goods that corporate power has to offer."[2]

Disney World is an enclosure under one management with a unified purpose that infuses all the exhibits and venues that form the variegated geography and architecture of the entire complex. In this sense, Disney World has an Orwellian structure. Yet the same principle can be extended to consumption in the wider capitalist economy, even where the multiple panoptic gazes are not under one management and may even be competitive with one another. Competition, which may be very real at the level of product lines, and rewards to shareholders, serves also to deepen the culture of consumption and thus the potential market for all competitors. As if in recognition of this shared interest, much of the personal information gathered by competitors is in effect pooled by information brokers and made accessible to anyone willing to pay. The decentered Panopticon is both fragmented and unified at the same time.

VERTICAL ISOLATION,
HORIZONTAL SOLIDARITY

The old, centered, hierarchical Panopticon depended on its capacity to isolate its subjects from one another. Bentham's prison was designed expressly to eliminate communication among prisoners; each was reduced to an apparently individualized relationship to the Inspector alone. Scientific management tried to appropriate control over labor as a means of breaking down crafts and craft unions that cemented worker solidarity. The dystopic regimes of Zamiatin and Orwell attempt systematically to replace horizontal relationships among the subjects with top-down, one-way command communications. In each of their famous novels, the hero's resistance is broken when he is forced through terror to betray the one to whom he has been closest; it is Winston Smith's betrayal of his lover Julia that finally allows him to love Big Brother unreservedly.

The new Panopticon primly eschews the crudities and brutalities of its predecessors. No more Room 101 at the end of the long corridor. But there is a structural similarity nonetheless. The new information technologies progressively individualize the consumer-subject. Indeed, marketing research is increasingly directed toward more and more minutely differentiating one group's tastes and preferences from another's, and eventually identifying individual (paying) consumer's preferences. Social solidarity is weakened as the consciousness of difference is assiduously evaluated, played on, and sold by the panoptic market. Subjects are isolated and civil society fragmented, but this is not achieved by the old, brass-knuckle and truncheon methods. Now, when the panoptic gaze addresses or interpellates subjects, it is on the basis of understanding their needs and serving their desires. So supple is this system that multiple producers compete with one another to catch the attention and the dollar of the sovereign consumer. Participatory surveillance is, of course, a much more powerful mechanism of consent than what came before.

A series of transformations in media and communications facilitate this process. The shift from broadcasting to narrowcasting in the electronic media offers ever more specialized entertainment vehicles for differentiated target markets. A few decades ago, there were only a handful of television channels. In the 1950s, viewers could flick the dial between CBS, NBC, and ABC. In other countries, the choices tended to be even more limited, and were to remain limited even longer. Major shows had mass audiences, and advertisers targeted as wide a market for their products as they could reach. The coming of cable and direct-broadcast satellites has dramatically transformed this landscape. As TV moves toward the 500-channel universe, specialty channels come to the fore. A channel featuring nothing but golf will have a relatively limited audience, but it is an audience very closely monitored by certain advertisers who recognize that the informational profile of golf enthusiasts offers a fit with their product lines. The more advertisers know about these viewers, the better they can serve this small niche market. The more they serve these viewers, the more they know about them.

The same trend is obvious in the print media. Mass-circulation newspapers have been declining in number for years, with takeovers and consolidation under chain ownership. There are periodic crises over the profit margins of dailies. At the same time, the 1990s have been a golden age for magazines—not the for the old mass market, all-things-to-all-people magazines such as the old *Life* or *Saturday Evening Post*, most of which have disappeared, but rather for special-interest magazines. On any magazine rack today, an Aladdin's Cave of treasures opens before prospective buyers, but each magazine is a treasure in the eyes of a particular segment of the public. Magazines beckon aficionados of the hip-hop music scene, fly fishing, mercenary soldiering, antique cars, line dancing, sadomasochism, poodles, the rare-coin trade. You name it, there is almost certainly a magazine or two to cater to your fancy. The ads attract more attention from readers than the articles. The audiences for these magazines know they will find ads for products that are precisely targeted at their special interests.

Radio too has followed this pattern. The phenomenon of Top 40 radio has been displaced by stations catering to more specialized music tastes: rock, rap, easy listening, golden oldies, country and western, ethnic, and so on, each with an appropriate array of advertisers. The latest medium of the internet extends this specialization to its ultimate. The number of specialized websites is limited only by the ingenuity and energy of individuals using the Net. At this point, advertisers have not really capitalized to any appreciable degree on the opportunities the Net provides for marketing to specialized audiences, but this is probably only a lag time that will sooner or later be made up.

With the fragmentation of mass audiences, less and less mass-audience programming is available. Certain highly hyped events such as the annual Super Bowl may still draw a relatively large audience and attract a number of first-run ads directed at a relatively wide audience (ads that are themselves reviewed in the media along with the game itself). Yet even Super Bowls and other major sports and entertainment events attract smaller shares of the TV audience than they once did. Certain shows, usually sitcoms, may establish a mass audience for a time by catching a particular demographic wave or a particular public mood. *Seinfeld* had a remarkable run for a time before its creator packed it in, perhaps anticipating and pre-empting inevitable decline. But more and more we can expect fragmented audiences following particular kinds of programs, in turn pursued by particular kinds of advertisers. The economics of the Panopticon dictate the result. But what of the cultural impact of this fragmentation on mass democracies? This is a very big question to which we can address, appropriately enough, only fragmentary answers.

THE MULTICULTURAL PANOPTICON

Consider how North American business has identified, targeted, and addressed various groups. Feminists have rightly attacked the image of women in advertising as sexual objects or accessories to men. At a time when men controlled most of the country's discretionary purchasing power, Madison Avenue had decided that "sex sells," and this meant "sexy women sell." Traditionally, in areas where women did make expenditures—household items, clothing, etc.—appeals were pitched to women that were in effect the mirror image of male-centered ads, that is, women as housewives/mothers or women trying to appear sexy for their men. In the age of mass marketing, one size had more or less to fit all. As women made their way further and higher into the work world, advertising began to change. As these changes coincided with the rapid proliferation of new information technologies and new marketing strategies, there was no simple turning of the page or reversal of role images. Instead, marketing began to target particular categories of the 'new' women with purchasing power as soon as they could be identified. Young attractive career women began to appear in various professional and business situations, always stylishly dressed, confident, sometimes offering smart advice to older male bosses, sometimes making decisions themselves. A variation of this is the new woman out in the work world who aggressively seeks out attractive men; the message: you can have it all, success and sex, too. But these images do not displace other, older images. Some of these are variations on old themes, such as the fast- and frozen-food ads targeting working mothers concerned to put dinner on the table for their families but no longer having the time to cook themselves, as stay-at-home moms were able to do. These ads offer reassurance to women trying to straddle two roles: you do both, they say, work during the day and then please your husband and kids when you all come home. Yet more traditional images continue, such as the male-centered sex object (drink our beer, have the woman; drive our car, drive the woman) or the devoted housewife and mother, and these periodically draw the fire of angry feminists who insist that nothing after all has really changed while such unsuitable role models continue to be propagated.

Such politically motivated criticisms (however laudable on their own terms) tend to miss the point. For business, the point, to turn Marx's well-known phrase on its head, is not to change the world but to understand it. The world now presents a much more variegated and diverse picture of women to the panoptic gaze. Are there women devoted above all to achieving success in their professional careers? Identify them, find out how they can be reached, how they think of themselves, how much money they have to spend, what they want to buy. Then design the products and design the ads that will draw them to your products. Then again, are there working women ambivalent about their role and feeling insecure about how their husbands and kids view them? Design the appropriate products to meet that insecurity, and design ads that feed on precisely that insecurity to ensure that they will buy them. At the same time, despite changing sex roles, there are still men who can be persuaded to part with their dollars by associating particular brands with willing female flesh. So babes and bimbos coexist in the advertising landscape with confident career women and earnest but troubled working moms. Capitalism is not in the business of spearheading social change, but its very lack of a social agenda means that its panoptic gaze can be very good at detecting stirrings of change that do occur, then capturing and shaping them as consumer demands that can be accommodated within the system. By differentiating the image of "woman," the panoptic sort also helps to disperse and fragment the potential political constituency of "women" into diffuse multiple constituencies of different kinds of women, with different affinities and different agendas. It does not create these constituencies, of course, but by encouraging and rewarding differentiation and individualization, it deepens tendencies to fragmentation already present.

In recent years, North American capitalism has begun to notice the potential of a "gay market." This could only happen once gays and lesbians began to come out of the closet and self-conscious gay and lesbian lifestyles and cultures began to appear in a fashion clearly visible to the straight world. Homophobic reactions remain in the wider society, of course, spurred by the AIDS panic and by evangelical and moral majoritarian anti-gay agitation. In a context of social change bristling with sociosexual anxieties, threats of continuing social sanctions and acts of gay-bashing violence, the identification and targeting of the gay market is a process fraught with pitfalls, on both sides. The panoptic gaze, which so often shows a positive, beneficial face to its subjects, in this case can appear dangerously ambiguous, even intimidating. In the very recent past—a past that infuses the present with menace—there was very much more coercive panoptic gaze searching for sexual "deviants" as security and employment risks, or as objects of blackmail (it was sometimes hard to clearly distinguish between these twin threats).

A 1998 case that drew national attention in the United States illustrates a continuing problem. Under the "don't ask, don't tell" policy that resulted from President Clinton's abortive effort to eliminate anti-gay discrimination in the U.S. military, a veteran naval officer with seventeen years honorable service was discharged. The officer used the word "gay" to describe his marital status on an America Online (the leading Internet service provider) member profile, which had been obtained by a civilian employee after she and the officer exchanged e-mail about a charity toy effort.[3] Although there was no personal identification in the profile to link the online alias with the naval officer, the Navy improperly obtained the identification from AOL, which later apologized for the disclosure.[4] However, the damage had been done.

In such a potentially threatening context, it is hardly surprising that the panoptic gaze scanning for an identifiable gay market may sometimes be met with more suspicion than welcome. On the other side, companies have to tread carefully in crafting advertising appeals so as not to raise anti-gay backlash among other customers. Despite these glitches, the advent of the gay market is no doubt an important step in the restructuring of the relationship between gays and lesbians and the larger society, perhaps toward an eventual disappearance of discrimination based on sexual orientation. The consumer Panopticon can legitimize previously marginalized groups by linking them and their disposable dollars to consumer capitalism, not as mass consumers whose specific identity is lost or hidden, but specifically in terms of what differentiates them from other groups and from the mainstream. In addressing gays *as gays*, not as mass consumers who happen to be gay in their off-hours, as it were, the panoptic gaze recognizes and validates their differences.

There are a number of points to be made about this process of panoptic recognition. It should never be forgotten that recognition is granted only in exchange for purchasing power. Marginalized groups without effective purchasing power remain marginalized. In the case of the gay market, it has been asserted that lesbians tend to lack purchasing power equivalent to that enjoyed by gay males, and that consequently the lesbian market has been relatively ignored. This observation could be extended to differentiation within the

gay male community as well. The panoptic gaze will light most fre-
quently and favorably on those gay men with the largest amount of
disposable income. Those in the professions, business, and entertainment are especially targeted for their visibility and affluence.
Class differences are thus accentuated and reinforced. Nor does
panoptic recognition come without specific conditions. Radical,
subversive, in-your-face gay politics are unlikely to be rewarded,
while more genial, accommodative, non-threatening "lifestyle" differences are welcomed. Participatory surveillance may be consensual and may downplay coercion, but it is in the end about
discipline and integration, not about rebellion and resistance. And
differentiation and fragmentation serve precisely these purposes.

Multiculturalism is currently trendy, contested, and eminently
political. To speak of a multicultural Panopticon might seem somewhat perverse. Multiculturalism is widely seen as a program of the
Left and is hotly opposed by conservatives. It is inherently unlikely
that corporate capitalism would champion challenges to its hegemony. Yet the cultural wars obscure a great deal more than they
illuminate. The sensitivity of the panoptic gaze to differences, even
to small, obscured differences is a central attribute of a creative,
adaptable, flexible conservatism.

With economic globalization, the double identity of the Panopticon as both competitive and unified proves a great strength: competition is the mechanism for the penetration of new markets, while
competition brings with it the universal acceptance of the culture of
consumption. The consumer Panopticon can spread its gaze globally precisely because it can adapt readily to local variations. A few
years ago, IBM ran a series of television ads portraying "Solutions
for a Small Planet" with cute clips of people in traditional and exotic
settings discussing (with English subtitles) various arcana relating
to the latest IBM technologies. Nuns in a European cloister, for instance, whisper to one another during prayers that they can't wait
to "surf the Net." Microsoft, which employs a large number of
Indian computer programmers and systems analysts for various
outsourced tasks, held a contest among Indian school children to
come up with technical solutions to particular programming problems. The winners were presented in a televised event with their

awards by no less than Bill Gates himself, watched by their proud parents, some in traditional Indian costume. The self-consciously multiracial and multicultural promotions of the clothing company Benetton (the "United Colours of Benetton") take this strategy so far as to occasionally arouse bursts of xenophobic outrage against suggestions of interracial sex or, in one celebrated case, the depiction of a black Queen of England. Benetton has also been accused of employing cheap labor in Third World sweatshops, thus nicely demonstrating that multicultural marketing can be based on multiculturalism in exploitation: in both cases, profitability is the primary criterion. In the 1950s and 1960s, critics warned of America's "Coca-Colonization" of the world. In the earlier era of mass marketing, a product like Coca-Cola, as standard as the Model T Ford, seemed emblematic of an imperialism in which an homogenized mass culture followed the corporate flag. In practice, Coca-Cola has been particularly skilled at adapting its products to the needs of different cultures. As Ronald Diebert writes of new information technologies, or "hypermedia":

> Through computer-based, digital-designed and operated manufacturing and advertising systems, hypermedia permit the production of "niche" products that are tailored to suit local conditions. With computer-assisted consumer profiles and other market-surveillance mechanisms, firms can then maintain a constant watch over disparate localities around the globe, enabling diversified responses to local conditions, as well as rapid adjustments in advertising campaigns to influence parochial consumer tastes. Even McDonald's—a symbol of capitalist homogenization if ever there was one—regularly changes many of its product and advertising characteristics to match local consumer profiles. In Japan, for example, it changed the name of its mascot from Ronald McDonald to Donald McDonald and the pronunciation of its name to "Makudonaldo," both of which are easier to pronounce for Japanese speakers.[6]

Multinational corporations have no problem with multiculturalism, as a factor in their workforces or as a description of global marketing strategies. The criss-crossing panoptic searchlights light up the cultural, linguistic, ethnic, and other particularities of their target markets, and flexible production can quickly respond with appropriately differentiated products and services. This, of course, assumes disposable incomes. Some parts of the globe remain relatively dark: most of Africa, parts of Asia, much of Latin America. The panoptic gaze scans but sees little of interest. Other parts, such as the former Soviet bloc economies, are in a flickering half-light: it is not yet clear whether they will come out of the darkness or fall back into it. But where markets are developed or developing, panoptic gazes scan incessantly.

In an influential article a few years ago, the Canadian political philosopher Charles Taylor wrote about multiculturalism as the politics of difference recognition.[7] Contrary to an older universalizing liberalism that strove to be color-blind, gender-blind, etc., multicultural politics seeks the recognition and validation of cultural difference as the basis of shared community. Capitalism's panoptic gaze seeks out and responds to difference. But what kind of "multiculturalism" is implied in this? Certainly critics who depict a purely white male Eurocentric commercialism imposing a ready-made racial/gender hierarchy and a Procrustean cultural structure on the rest of the world fail to grasp the capacity of panoptic practices to adapt and embed themselves in multiple environments. At the same time, there is a profound difference between the multiculturalism of informational capitalism and multiculturalism as a philosophy of social and political change. Capitalism recognizes and constitutes people as *consumers*, but not as *citizens*. Multicultural consumption is not multicultural citizenship: there is a world of difference.

Earlier Panopticons always engendered resistance. Today's Panopticon is more subtle, more flexible, more participatory, more consensual. But perfect social control still exists only in the imagination. The genetically engineered consent of Huxley's *Brave New World* might appear closer to us than the brutality of Orwell's grim police state, but the proximity is superficial. The charms of consumption are seductive, but there are too many people by far — millions in the Third World, but too many as well in the "developed" world — who are excluded from benefits, and thus from the panoptic gaze. Most have always lacked the passport that allows entry in the first instance: money. Others have been expelled from the charmed circle as "risks"; with the rapid acceptance around the globe of the neoliberal economic agenda, they are even being ex-

pelled from the secondary fall-back surveillance system of state welfare. Others sense instinctively the politically limited and culturally
impoverished reality that lies behind the title of "sovereign consumer." Resistance takes the forms of *struggles for citizenship* that
cannot be contained or managed through recognition as consumers. And the ultimate irony is that the very technologies that support
and enable capitalism's panoptic gaze also empower citizenship
struggles. I turn to the democratic promise of the new technologies
in the following chapter.

THE AGE OF MULTIDIRECTIONAL SURVEILLANCE

As high-tech enhanced surveillance intensifies from the top down, it
is also true that high-tech enhanced surveillance intensifies from the
bottom up. Television began as a top-down, one-way media, in
which the only effective audience participation was through rigidly
selected and controlled studio audiences (often replaced in sitcoms
by automated "canned" laugh tracks), or through the depersonalized mass program ratings system. TV has been adapted for one-
way surveillance through closed-circuit security cameras scanning
everything from apartment lobbies to parking garages to office cor-
ridors. This same basic technology in the form of the hand-held
video camera has become a tool for cheap, mobile guerilla countersurveillance. Much of this use is trivial, non-political, and quickly
absorbed and utilized by the media as commodified entertainment:
America's Funniest Home Videos.[8] But there are examples of sometimes explosive political use of video as well. The beating of Rodney
King by the L.A. police, captured on video by a solitary witness,
became the basis for a major racial conflict and urban riots across
American cities. In Canada, videos taken by participants in training
sessions of an elite airborne regiment of the Canadian armed forces
and shown on national television so shocked the public by the dis-
play of racism, brutality, and degradation that the regiment was ordered disbanded by the Minister of Defense. In another Canadian
case, rioting prisoners in a women's correctional institute were disciplined by being forced to strip and run a gauntlet of guards; the

entire event was captured on a video that made its way into the media, forcing an official inquiry and finally the resignation of the responsible prison official. In all these cases, behavior by public servants that in the past was practiced out of sight, out of mind, suddenly became public knowledge—with serious consequences. Nor is it always guerilla countersurveillance from below: Richard Nixon's secretive penchant for recording conversations in the Oval Office ensnared him in the White House tapes fiasco that helped drive him out of office under imminent threat of impeachment. The technology itself, rather than human agency, may be the culprit, as in the case of the White House e-mails implicating various Reagan administration officials in the Iran-Contra affair: the conspirators failed to inform themselves properly of some of the automatic retention features of the White House e-mail system, and the frantic electronic shredding that accompanied the massive paper-shredding operations did not succeed in erasing all records of sensitive communications. Eventually, through a lawsuit brought by a public interest group, thousands of computer tapes and even 135 computer hard drives from the National Security Council staff, were preserved for the public record.[9]

One of the immediate effects of this era of multidirectional surveillance is to place public figures in a constant remorseless glare of publicity directed at their private lives as well as their public roles, fed by media hunger for uncovering sex and sleaze among the powerful. Take the preposterous spectacle in early 1998 of the Presidency of the United States held hostage for weeks to the question of whether the President did or did not have sex with a consenting adult White House intern—sparked in the first instance by the clandestine taping and subsequent public exposure of what the intern believed were private conversations with a "friend." The Monica Lewinsky affair (perhaps we might dub this the first "virtual affair") represents a kind of *reductio ad absurdum* of democratic accountability. The precipitous rise of this so-called scandal to the top of the media agenda (trumping, for instance, an historic visit of the Pope to Fidel Castro's Cuba) was driven in part by proliferating rumor-as-news on the Internet. The latter might seem democratic and participatory by contrast to the highly structured and heavily institutionalized world of the electronic and print media. The same networking that has been breaking down traditional corporate structures is showing up in media enterprise as well, described as *disintermediation*. As Jack Shafer explains:

> In the world of electronic commerce, you hear a lot about "disinter-mediation"—the elbowing out of middlemen and distributors by the Web, which directly connects manufacturers with consumers. It is premature to herald the disintermediation of the news business by Web independents who leapfrog editors, libel attorneys and conventional journalistic standards. But . . . anybody who has an Internet connection and something original to say can reach a global audience. Sensing this disintermediation in the works, the old media have expanded their profile on the Web . . . Already, electronic commerce mavens are talking about "reintermediation," in which a new breed of Web middleman will rise to make sense out of the chaos wrought by disintermediation. As the technology of the Web evolves, Internet devices will become as ubiquitous as telephones. Every newspaper will have the potential to break news as fast as a television station. Every television station will have the potential to become a newspaper.[10]

The downside of this is that at present there exist few professional standards of journalism or ethics on the internet. Indeed, it is the amateur, grass-roots nature of the Net that lend it its particular populist cachet. But the obverse of amateurism is irresponsibility. Like bad currency driving out good, Net-driven rumors in the Lewinsky affair impelled the mainstream media, led by the cable news networks avid for instant news, to rush into print and on screen with unconfirmed rumors of their own, many of which had to be retracted within days or even hours.

There is something inherently invidious about intensive surveillance of people in the public sector while wealth and power in the private sector are given less intrusive scrutiny. Because democratic politicians are accountable to the voters, their private lives are held by many to be public property. Corporate barons, accountable if at all only to their own shareholders, are permitted private behavior that might rouse media moralizing if it involved political figures. In an era in which states are seen to be in retreat before the advance of a globalizing private sector, the trivialization of the public space as soap opera or trash TV would seem to hasten the denigration of the public in favor of the private, and the displacement of politics by markets and states by corporations. In fact it is becoming increasingly difficult to distinguish the "real" world of politics from the "fantasy" world of TV, a process accelerated by politicians anxious to plug into the public's TV-inspired dreamscape. Ronald Reagan spent eight years in the White House playing one last Hollywood role, this time as President of the United States, and according to the polls he did a convincing job. Former Vice President Dan Quayle attacked TV sitcom character Murphy Brown for having a baby out of wedlock (for all the world, as if Murphy Brown were a Democratic opponent). And then to complete the circle, Dan Quayle became himself a character on a subsequent Murphy Brown show. So Bill and Hillary, instead of being the President and First Lady, become like characters in a soap — and Monica, "the other woman," just happens to hail from Beverly Hills, zip code 90210, which just happens to echo the name of a soap featuring glamorous young people and frenetic infidelity. The Lewinsky affair hit the public consciousness just a few weeks after a Hollywood comedy, *Wag The Dog*, hit the nation's theaters. In this film, a President, caught out in a sexual misdemeanor in the White House, is saved by a spin doctor and a film producer who script and stage a phony war as a media event to distract the public's attention — successfully. Seemingly following the script, President Clinton promptly began escalating a conflict with that all-purpose, all-weather useful enemy of America, Saddam Hussein. Coming soon to a theater near you: *Desert Storm, The Sequel*. News is packaged as entertainment and entertainment is news. As we wander farther and farther into the enchanted heart of Neverneverland, there is less and less TV time for boring policy wonks who want to talk about poverty, health care, and environmental protection. When Clinton fled the scandal-beleaguered White House for a tour of the heartland to talk about the economic good news of low unemployment, low inflation, and low interest rates, a CNN news reader commented that it would be interesting to see if the President could succeed in "distracting" the voters!

Under a sheen of populist self-congratulation, "democratic" countersurveillance conceals a paradox at its very heart. Liberalism suggests that the answer to intrusive surveillance lies in the defense of *privacy*, in creating legal and moral barriers to protect the individual against the myriad of prying eyes, or at least to minimize their penetration as much as reasonably possible. Hence such bureaucratic devices as privacy boards and commissioners, voluntary codes of corporate conduct, and legal screens to block or slow the flow of data-matching and data-mining. Laws are passed restricting access to data on private citizens, usually in tandem with freedom of information statutes. Here is the paradox: privacy protection is inherently in tension with freedom of information. Indeed, in practice many seeking access to government records have found that the most impenetrable barrier they face is the protection of the privacy of so-called third parties, an ironic outcome, given that both privacy and freedom-of-information laws were promoted by groups seeking to limit the surveillant power of the bureaucratic state. Countersurveillance for democratic purposes tends to be just as intolerant of privacy as surveillance by the state and corporations. Whether such countersurveillance is carried out by investigative journalists, academics, or by public-interest groups or social movements, and whatever the specific political results, countersurveillance has the paradoxical result of strengthening the surveillance-mindedness and the surveillance-tolerance of the society. At the same time, privacy protection often appears as reactionary or as inherently suspicious: surely only those with something to hide will seek to protect themselves from public scrutiny? That, of course, is precisely the conservative defense of surveillance itself.

Surveillance that is decentered and multidirectional may open greater opportunities for resistance. It may also contribute to the general decline of the legitimacy of large organizations, among which the state will be the first in line, although not likely the last. Yet another is the blurring of the line between reality and fantasy, between news and entertainment. With everyone and everything brought on camera and on tape for everyone else's prurient curiosity, the very idea of a life dedicated purely to public service becomes not merely suspect, but difficult to even grasp as a concept. J. Edgar Hoover bugged and spied on hotel bedrooms used by Martin Luther King, Jr., and amassed dossiers on King's sexual infidelities in an attempt to discredit his historic civil rights campaign. Hoover failed. (And Hoover himself fell pry to posthumous voyeurs who allege that he was homosexual and—with little evidence if any—that he was a transvestite in private.) But when surveillance becomes multidirectional and no longer the preserve of the Federal Bureau of Investigation, privacy begins to be generally seen as little more than a barrier to the public's right to know. It would be foolish to imagine that this indecent attention will be confined to peering only at the rich and famous. Andy Warhol said that everyone would have their fifteen minutes of media fame—perhaps better compressed now to fifteen seconds. But what if that fifteen minutes is not fame but infamy, fifteen minutes of being stripped naked before *America's Most Censorious Home Videos*? Two-way transparency in the city of glass might have been an eighteenth-century dream of Rousseau, who naively imagined that the purity of his soul, so apparent to him, would be equally apparent to all others. It might turn out to be a twenty-first-century nightmare.

As the *New York Times* columnist Russell Baker only half-humorously writes:

> George Orwell, who created Big Brother in his novel *1984*, envisioned the ever-watching monster as a political tyrant . . . Living in an age of tyrants, he thought 20th-century technology could produce indestructible political dictators. He was wrong about this. It was the new technology that made tyranny on the Soviet model obsolete.
>
> Still, there are tyrannies and tyrannies. A world in which surveillance is inescapable cannot be everyone's dream of a democratic Paradise. And the surveillance is not confined to officially authorized busybodies like the FBI, Kenneth Starr and your local cop with his radar gun. It was a private citizen with his own video camera who photographed the Los Angeles police beating Rodney King. Such cameras are everywhere nowadays. Pick your nose and you could wind up in *The National Enquirer*. Stand in the backyard spanking your disobedient 5-year-old and you could end up doing hard time for child abuse. . . .
>
> I hear it said that people who have nothing to hide need not fear this strangulating technology of surveillance. And where are they, these people with nothing to hide?[12]

That is a tough question. And in the age of decentered, multidirectional surveillance, there is another tough question: What happens when there is nowhere to hide?

NOTES TO CHAPTER 6

1. Andrew O'Hagan, *The Missing* (N.Y.: New Press, 1997), cited by Neal Ascherson, "Lost," *The New York Review of Books*, XLV:1, 15 January 1998, 31.

2. Clifford D. Shearing and Philip C. Stenning, "From the Panopticon to Disney World: The Development of Discipline," in Anthony. N. Doob and Edward L. Greenspan, eds., *Perspectives in Criminal Law: Essays in Honour of John Ll. J. Edwards* (Toronto: Canada Law Book, 1984), 347.

3. Lisa Napoli, "Sailor Says Navy Is Using AOL Profile to Oust Him," *New York Times*, 9 January 1998.

4. Lisa Napoli, "AOL Admits Error in Sailor's Case," *New York Times*, 21 January 1998.

5. A few years ago, an Australian film, *The Coca-Cola Kid*, depicted an all-American sales executive parachuted into Australia to put a local soft-drink competitor out of business. He immediately sets out to exploit Australian aboriginal music in a Coke sales pitch that identifies the product with indigenous culture.

6. Ronald J. Diebert, *Parchment, Printing and Hypermedia: Communications in World Order Transformation* (N.Y.: Columbia University Press, 1997), 144–45.

7. Charles Taylor, "The Politics of Recognition," in Amy Gutmann, ed., *Multiculturalism and the Politics of Recognition* (Princeton University Press, 1994), 25–74.

8. In the 1960s, the same idea was utilized in a more hierarchically controlled setting. *Candid Camera* planned and directed elaborate visual jokes into which innocent persons were lured and then laughed at by a TV audience complicit in the charade. *America's Funniest* on the other hand is dependent for its content on contributions from grass-roots video-makers, often using fortuitously amusing footage from home movies shot for private rather than public or commercial purposes. In many cases, the videos may well have been planned and staged, but the point is that this time the artifice is populist and democratic, as opposed to the manipulative and rather authoritarian overtones of the earlier generation. The difference is simply the wide diffusion of the hand-held video camera.

9. Tom Blanton, ed., *White House E-Mail: The Top Secret Computer Messages the Reagan/Bush White House Tried to Destroy* (N.Y.: The New Press, 1995).

10. Jack Shafer, "The Web Made Me Do It," *New York Times*, 15 February 1998.

11. Jean Starobinski, *Jean-Jacques Rousseau: La transparence et l'obstacle* (Paris: Editions Gallimard, 1971).

12. Russell Baker, "Quiet, Quiet, Louie, There's a Bug in That Martini Olive," *New York Times*, 13 February 1998.

7—Big Brother Outsourced: The Globalized Panopticon

We have described throughout this book some of the impacts of the new information technologies on power and how it is exercised. We have looked at the transformations of the concept of the Panopticon and of surveillance as a mechanism of social control. We have discussed the rise of the network society as a new paradigm of political, social, and economic organization and a few of the cultural implications of this change. Most of this discussion has focussed on liberal democracies in North America and Western Europe. But the new information technologies are universalizing, and the panoptic techniques pioneered and developed in the West will continue to spread. The network society is being globalized—indeed, its inner dynamic is precisely toward globalization. What can we foresee of the shape of power in the networked world?

VIRTUAL FEUDALISM?

Abbe Mowshowitz has described a possible future for the networked world that he calls "virtual feudalism."[1] Beginning with an analysis of the underlying technological trends that have facilitated the "virtual organization" as an efficient new organizational form, he goes on to speculate that structural changes comparable in their depth and scope to those that accompanied the transformation of feudalism to capitalism will accompany the new revolution. He points to trends already evident in traditional authority structures, particularly the family and the nation-state. In regard to the latter, he posits either its "decline" or its "end"; if the nation-state does not disappear, he seems to suggest, it will become virtually irrelevant.

Many others have similarly predicted the decline and fall of the nation-state. What distinguishes Mowshowitz's vision of the future is his striking depiction of an ironic historical "recurrence": the "new" post-nation-state era, he suggests, will look much like the pre-capitalist world of feudalism. Just as the emerging market eroded and ultimately gutted the feudal authority system, so too the economic capacities of the flexible virtual organization in the new networked world will erode and ultimately gut the authority relations of the world organized by nation-states. With the decline of state resources and thus of state power, private centers of economic power will gradually assume political power. As in medieval feudalism, the basic functions of government will come to be exercised by private parties. This is not just a change in the names of the providers of public services. With the shift in function will come a shift in power and legitimacy. Private parties will exercise authority in their own name, not in the name of a law that transcends their own power. This is the essence of feudalism.[2]

The picture he paints of this new feudalism is not pretty, involving widespread impoverishment of the millions of people excluded from the benefits of the information economy, in many cases no longer even required for cheap labor, and increasingly denied social benefits from hollowed-out and penniless national states. Grotesquely exaggerated disparities of wealth are not alleviated by even moderate redistribution, because the logic of profit-maximization linked to political power excludes macro-social in favor of micro-economic rationality. Consequently, disorder is likely to be widespread and to have to be contained by private force.[3] Relatively secure centers will coexist with lawless areas—a geography perhaps already prefigured in the contrast between inner-city desolation and gated affluent suburbia in late twentieth-century America. At the very least, there will likely be a prolonged period of disorder and anarchy paralleling the Dark Ages before the Middle Ages, when feudal relations became more stable and ordered.

Mowshowitz does not spell out the full logic of his feudal analogy, indeed he tends to shrink from some of its darker implications. But the imagery of feudalism has a power that rather overreaches his deliberately limited use of it as a heuristic device. We have in the West an historical memory of the Middle Ages as a time of oppressive hierarchy, obscurantism and superstition, witchcraft and warlords, the Inquisition and the Black Death. To imagine a reversion in the twenty-first century to the conditions of a thousand years earlier is to imagine a descent into madness or senility. In this sense, the vision of "virtual feudalism" has, whatever Mowshowitz's intentions, the makings of a twenty-first-century dystopia as vividly threatening as the twentieth-century dystopia of *1984* or *We*. The ultimate centralization of all economic and political power in the imaginary totalitarian state gives way to the ultimate decentralization of economic and political power in virtual feudalism; the one is no less chilling than the other. But is it any more realistic? After all, we did have real totalitarian states in this century, they inflicted staggering violence and suffering; but they fell well short of the totalitarian dream, and in the end they could not sustain themselves. How likely is that virtual feudalism will emerge as a world system, as a global organizing principle?

Mowshowitz's model does have a number of factors going for it. Looking at the trends of the networked globe that are emerging, we can isolate the decentering of power and authority, the detachment of sovereignty from territory, the erosion of many of the traditional prerogatives of the nation-state and the blurring of lines between the public and private sectors, the transformation of work and the creation of an underclass of the apparently permanently unemployed and unemployable, growing disparities of wealth and poverty not only on a global scale but also within the so-called rich nations, the growth of private security and private justice. The existence of these and other trends would seem to support the possibility that a new feudalism will emerge. There is always the danger of assuming that present trends will simply continue in a linear fashion; that the future will be like the present, only more so. Significantly, however, Mowshowitz has constructed his projections not only on contemporary trends, but on the underlying structural basis of these trends, specifically the new organizational forms enabled and promoted by the new information technologies. These new forms suggest decentering, dispersal, and privatization. This could point in the direction of "feudalism" with dispersed centers of economic and political power and a hierarchy very steep at the bottom but somewhat flatter at the top as shifting congeries of powerful "barons" (corporations?) challenge the authority of relatively weak "kings" (states?).

Although persuasive at first glance, this image of the future loses its clarity the closer and longer one examines it. As Mowshowitz himself points out, actual feudalism was based on the immobile resource of land, while virtual feudalism is based on an organizational form enabled by the transformation of information into a commodity that flows globally:

> Virtual feudalism shares the political features of classical feudalism, but its economic base is abstract wealth, and the social system based upon it may be very fluid. The central institution of virtual feudalism will be the virtual fief, rather than the manor or landed estate of European feudalism. Assets will be distributed on a global basis as "virtual resources," i.e., the particular form of abstract wealth may change from moment to moment depending on the institution's financial needs and market conditions.[4]

This is a more damaging qualification than he seems ready to admit. It was the very immobility of land as resource that permitted the decentered authority structure of feudalism, and provided the condition for the relative stability of the social relations of feudalism for the centuries when this form predominated. It is very difficult to imagine even the minimal degree of stability required for the persistence of virtual feudalism as a distinct system when fluidity, flexibility, and real-time global flows of abstract wealth are at the very heart of the organizational form being proposed. "Feudalism" as a metaphor seems singularly inapt when a system rooted in fixity, tradition, custom, and usage is being compared with one posited on febrile change, constant liquidation and recreation, and movement almost for the sake of movement. Perhaps Mowshowitz is providing an inadvertent exemplar of Marshall McLuhan's gnomic warning against driving into the future while steering by the rearview mirror.

BRINGING THE STATE BACK IN

There are more immediate problems with Mowshowitz's analysis of the transition to virtual feudalism. He pays no attention whatever to what economists call "externalities," specifically, to the environmental effects of production organized, as he suggests, "feudally" by private parties unchecked by regulation. "Abstract" wealth is all very well, but even the networked, information economy is engaged in production that is not abstract, but material: products that feed, house, warm, cool, clothe, transport, entertain and doctor, etc. Material production and the consumption of resources have environmental consequences, as most of us are only too well aware, and these consequences are often cumulative and very, very costly indeed—even fatal. A future globe in which all political and regulatory power is effectively dispersed to an evanescent multitude of profit-seeking private parties with short organizational life spans and limited institutional identities, each pursuing immediate economic self-interest, is surely a prescription for global environmental degradation on a life-threatening scale: a macro-irrationality of staggering proportions.

This is not to say that it could not happen, but by not even factoring the environmental impact into his model, Mowshowitz leaves a very large gap in its functionality. I would suggest that this very gap is already being recognized in the contemporary global political economy, and is actually pushing states, otherwise in retreat, to assert a serious presence in global authority and decision-making. Environmental degradation is in no one's interest in the larger sense, even if in the narrow micro-economic sense, profit-seeking activity that produces environmental devastation is "rational." So long as regulation of self-destructive behavior is universal, so that no one party loses competitive advantage by accepting limitations on its activity in relation to other, unregulated competitors, there is no real loss, only general betterment. This means global regulation.

There exists, however, only one site for effective enforcement of environmental rules: the nation-state. Global regulation requires binding agreements among governments—with teeth, which is to say, individual states with the strength and will to compel private actors within their jurisdictions to comply. Hence, the tentative steps in the 1990s toward state-to-state cooperation to control damage to the ozone layer and greenhouse gas emissions. How well these specific agreements will work in practice is debatable, but the enactment in principle of cooperation among (relatively strong) states in enforcing global environmental rules is likely only the beginning for more such agreements in other areas of common concern and common danger. The absence of any notice of this dimension in the model of virtual feudalism is a grave weakness. After all, classical feudalism fell into a terminal crisis in the fourteenth century when centuries of poor ecological practices in agriculture culminated in massive famine, followed shortly by the devastation of the Black Death. Feudal institutions could neither contain nor manage such "natural" catastrophes, and the resultant era of bitter class struggle, of peasants' and artisans' revolts, helped bring about the decline and fall of the feudal mode of production. Needless to say, contemporary capitalism dwarfs feudalism in its capacity to threaten the global ecological balance, and thus its own security.

Another grave weakness in the virtual feudalism model, as in many other extrapolations of a globally networked future, is the inert role assigned the losers in the globalized economy. At most, those who are impoverished or victimized are seen as presenting problems of crime and disorder, to be dealt with by—largely private—security. There does seem to be something irrational about the headlong drive of neoliberals to reduce and even eliminate social welfare programs. After all, with permanent long-term unemployment removing many (especially young male) workers from the discipline of the workplace, welfare programs, with their bureaucratic controls over clients, represent a kind of secondary surveillance system to monitor individuals. When the risk-aversive Panopticon further cuts the unreliable off credit, yet another grip over people on the margins is loosened. Not surprisingly, such people are more likely to end up under the coercive—and very costly—discipline of the prison system, which has been swelling into one of the biggest growth areas in the United States. Even if prisons in the United States are being rapidly privatized, they are licenced and regulated by the state; it is clear that the private sector is generally not prepared or even structured to assume, via individual corporations, the full social costs of police, courts, and prisons.

Just as enforcement of rules is a missing link in the virtual feudal model, so too the enforcement of security (and thus sovereignty) that Mowshowitz rather glibly assigns his private parties does not stand up to close scrutiny. It is true that private security has already surpassed public security in North America in terms of the allocation of resources and personnel, and that to a surprising degree private justice within private organizations, worked out without the intervention of the formal legal process, has been supplanting the police and the courts.[5] But these trends have been happening within the confines of national boundaries, and within an existing framework of public security and public justice that permits degrees of autonomy for private security that are, in effect, licensed or delegated, within limits, by the public authority.

The problem of the social costs of crime and disorder among the permanent underclass is not the only blind spot in the neoliberal agenda. The idea that economic globalization will proceed to its ultimate logical conclusion without any effective resistance, on a global scale, of those marginalized and excluded from the benefits is quite absurd, and flies in the face of history. Nor is there any reason to imagine, along with the bland theorists of corporate hegemony, that only the capitalist enterprise will be able to grasp and successfully exploit the new organizational forms that the new information technologies encourage and reward.

"WE'RE WATCHING YOU, BIG BROTHER!"

In early 1998, it was reported that "In their most networked action yet, . . . supporters [of the Zapatista or EZLN rebels] hacked into a Mexican government Web site and plastered it with pictures of the rebels' revolutionary namesake, Emiliano Zapata. Part of the rebel message, posted on the Finance Ministry homepage, read: "We're watching you, big brother!"[6] The Zapatistas have been described as "the first informational guerilla movement"[7] This particular action has nice symbolic content, but perhaps little substance. It does point, however, to the movement's remarkable capacity to network on a global scale (using the Internet, television, etc.) while carrying out a peasant rebellion against the Mexican government and its neoliberal globalization policies. The global communications linkages the Zapatistas established probably prevented the Mexican government from dealing with the rebellion in the time-honored fashion of massive repression, precipitating the unusual alternative of negotiations. As Castells explains, "actual warfare was not their strategy. The Zapatistas used arms to make a statement, then parlayed the possibility of their sacrifice in front of the world media to force a negotiation and advance a number of reasonable demands which, as opinion polls seem to indicate, found widespread support in Mexican society at large. . . . The Zapatistas' ability to communicate with the world, and with Mexican society, and to capture the imagination of people and of intellectuals, propelled a local, weak insurgent group to the forefront of world politics."[8] And the support networks set up outside Mexico have been important. Chase Manhattan reported to investors that the Mexican government would have to annihilate the rebel movement to restore investor confidence. Immediately, an American support net reproduced the text on the Net and mobilized a powerful backlash against Chase among "ethical" investors concerned about democracy as well as their rate of return.[9]

Another, less well-known, example of networking for resistance comes from the James Bay Cree Indians of northern Quebec, and their successful campaign against the "James Bay Two" or "Great Whale" hydroelectric megaproject, promoted avidly for years by the government of Quebec and its hydroelectric utility. *HydroQuébec* is a proud centerpiece of the new Quebec nationalism. The earlier James Bay One development was a source of great pride for Quebec aspirations: a vast, technologically sophisticated megaproject that connected Quebec with global export markets for hydroelectric power—a symbol of Quebec's capacity to construct a modern state and economy run by *Québécois*. James Bay Two would be the continuation of this development and, after a secessionist party took power in 1994, it would also be a symbol of Quebec's resolve and capacity to break free from the constraints of Canadian federalism and take its place in the global economy.

From the perspective of the Aboriginal people of Quebec's north, the James Bay development appears very differently. It is an aggressive, imperialistic thrust of capitalist European "civilization" into the very heart of native land and the native economy. Hydroelectric dams radically transform the landscape itself, flooding ancient lands, rerouting rivers and streams, slicing and severing the migration paths of wildlife and disrupting hunting and trapping patterns. Entire communities have to be uprooted and "relocated." At first glance, this process appears as the very paradigm of modernity impinging on traditional ways of life. The hydro grid advances relentlessly across the primeval landscape, subduing all, man and beast, tree and river, in its path. Nature is transformed by technological alchemy into power which turns the engines of capitalist industry. Particularities, traditions, and irregularities are forced into the straight rigid lines of empire that transport this power to foreign markets, thus connecting and subordinating Cree lands to the networks of the global economy.

The James Bay Cree mobilized a major resistance movement to the plans for stage two. This was not only another forlorn last-ditch stand by an endangered people. A sophisticated international publicity campaign was mounted to capture world opinion. U.S. political personality Robert Kennedy, Jr., and a leading American publicity firm were enlisted. The Cree *networked*, building on international environmental groups with experience and expertise in gaining access to global communications systems. Publicity highly unfavorable to the Quebec government was generated in American and Western European media. The legislature of New York (the major export market for Quebec hydroelectric power) was persuaded to refuse to purchase power generated by the Great Whale. The Quebec government, faced with hearings in Washington where the Cree confronted Quebec spokespersons in an atmosphere generally hostile to Quebec, finally backed down and shelved the Great Whale project.

Threatened by the enclosing networks of global capitalism (the power grid), the Aboriginal people of northern Quebec fought back by networking with international environmental groups. To be sure, the battle for Aboriginal rights has hardly been won in this one successful skirmish, but the strategy of resistance is interesting and offers one model for the information age.

Another recent example of networking for resistance is the successful campaign against the Multilateral Agreement on Investment (MAI). This proposed agreement, hammered out in secret by governments under the aegis of the Organization for Economic Cooperation and Development (OECD), would have instituted binding rules on treatment of foreign investors.[10] Everything was proceeding smoothly behind closed doors, until a Canadian public-interest advocacy group got its hands on a draft of the agreement. As one reporter describes the subsequent events:

> High-powered politicians had reams of statistics and analysis on why a set of international investing rules would make the world a better place. They were no match, however, for a global band of grassroots organizations, which, with little more than computers and access to the Internet, helped derail a deal. Indeed, international negotiations have been transformed after [the] successful rout of the Multilateral Agreement on Investment (MAI) by opposition groups, which—alarmed by the trend toward economic globalization—used some globalization of their own to fight back.[11]

The Canadians, many of whom had previously been involved in unsuccessful campaigns against the implementation of the Canada–U.S. Free Trade Agreement of 1989 and the subsequent North American Free Trade Agreement (NAFTA), had learned from the shortcomings of their earlier, pre-cyberspace campaigns. This time they linked with online groups in other countries, such as the Malaysia-based Third World Network. Every bit of new information about the secret draft agreement was instantly made available, and critical analysis of the MAI's implications for national governments sped quickly around the globe. Information gathered in one country that might prove embarrassing to a government in another was quickly publicized. Caught in their own secrecy, national governments were crippled in their capacity to respond. Indeed, nongovernmental groups became better informed about the details and implications of the MAI than many of the government ministers they were confronting. A global wave of protest engulfed the OECD negotiators, who admitted defeat in early 1998. "'This is the first successful Internet campaign by non-governmental organizations," said one diplomat involved in the negotiations. "It's been very effective.'" Having blocked the draft agreement, the same groups are anxious to play a more positive role in the future, to make constructive proposals for what ought to be in trade agreements, for example, rather than simply opposing what government negotiators propose. As one of the Canadians active in the campaign put it: "We're against this model of economic globalization. But the global village, the idea of coming together and working together, is a great dream."[12]

THE BISHOP OF NOWHERE
AND EVERYWHERE

For another take on how new information technologies are spurring new forms of resistance, we might look at the oldest continuous hierarchical authority structure in the world, the Roman Catholic Church. No other organization comes even remotely close to the Catholic Church for longevity; originating at the time of the Roman Empire, the church flourished throughout the feudal epoch and continues through the end of the second millennium undiminished, and indeed more widespread than ever. In two thousand years, the hierarchy has learned a thing or two about maintaining its authority. Confronted with turbulent and troublesome priests, the Vatican learned long ago that there were techniques more effective than outright repression. One was appointment to a non-existent diocese of "Partenia," notionally located in the Atlas Mountains in the midst of the Sahara Desert of North Africa. Partenia was literally nowhere, a diocese without a church and without any faithful, in short, a useful figment of the hierarchy's imagination into which bothersome clerics could be consigned, to vanish without trace but without the nuisance of an inquisition and punishment. And so it was used for centuries, until Bishop Jacques Gaillot in 1995.

Gaillot is the former bishop of Evreux, France, and a cleric of pronouncedly left-wing views which diverge from Papal doctrine on many points. Instead of keeping his views private, Gaillot publicly expressed solidarity with groups and causes from which the Church had officially maintained its distance. The Pope appointed Gaillot bishop of Partenia, and no doubt expected that he had heard the last of him. It had worked for centuries, but apparently no longer in the age of cyberspace. Jacques Gaillot simply set up Partenia as a website on the Internet. The diocese of nowhere now found a home in the medium that is nowhere—and everywhere. A diocese in the bleak mountains of the Sahara was in the past as silent as the desert sands, but a virtual diocese in cyberspace gives the bishop a voice that can be heard everywhere, and a faithful that can be gathered from all corners of the earth. Thus, in early 1998, any visitor to Partenia could read the Bishop's thoughts on taking part in a demonstration of the unemployed against the French government—and could e-mail their own reactions to the Bishop. One French author was reported as claiming religious ramifications of cyberspace: "The mind of God is imitated by the virtual structure of the Internet, where the difference between physical actuality and real existence has at last been breached."[13] Not to get carried away: the Roman Catholic Church is hardly shaken to its foundations by this particular on-line dissidence. Yet there is challenge to hierarchical authority implicit in the use of the new technology that might perhaps have sent a tiny shiver down a back or two in the hierarchy.

There are a number of other examples of political resistance enabled by new information technologies. The popular struggle against the Slobodan Milosevic regime in Serbia was given a boost by Internet connections. Not only did this provide wider support networks for the dissidents, but when the regime censored the domestic media, the movement could continue to communicate with the public via the Net, which Milosevic could not control. Embattled labor unions in South Korea and the student movement in China that led up the Tiananmen Square massacre (at that time communicating mainly by faxes) are other examples. Less dramatically but perhaps more importantly in the longer run, grass-roots movements in many Third World countries have employed the Net as a tool for organization, and are finding that global networking can provide useful real-time links to a multitude of non-governmental organizations involved in development assistance and to worker, peasant, and indigenous people's groups like themselves in other countries. Even in countries in which there are very few computers, and not even many telephone lines, a small number of activists with access to the technology can act as a communications funnel for the wider movement—a funnel that works both ways, bringing information of the wider world down to the local area, but also channeling local information upward.

No notice of the political implications of the Net would be complete without recognition of the role it has played in furthering the propaganda of extreme right-wing neo-nazi and racist groups in Europe and North America. Some specialize in Holocaust denial, others in passing on practical information on lethal bomb making and other terrorist devices. Groups such as the American militias keep in touch with one another via the Net, as do neo-fascists in various European countries. A U.N.-sponsored conference in Geneva in late 1997 heard one monitor indicate that the "number of hate sites has nearly doubled to 600 in the last year . . . There are at least 94 sites promoting a racial hierarchy that would classify Europeans by skin color, religion, ethnicity and even preferred language . . ." At the time, he counted ". . . 87 neo-Nazi sites, 35 white supremacist sites and 51 sites espousing terrorism."[14] Not surprisingly, this kind of hate propaganda has led to calls for Net censorship—and the usual perplexity about how to do with this without undermining freedom of expression and without impairing the free-wheeling spontaneity that has characterised the development of the Internet. Laws already in place controlling hate propaganda against identifiable groups can of course be invoked against website authors as readily as against print publishers—in theory. In practice, authorship and site location on the global Web remain difficult to nail down within boundary-limited legal jurisdictions. For those who see the new technologies as offering the opportunity to advance progressive political agendas, the prevalence of fascist and racist agitation offers a sobering lesson: the Net has no inherent political color. It does offer an ironic demonstration of the subversive potential of the technologies. Fascism and racism are now ideological expressions outside the legitimate mainstream of Western political discourse. The aptitude that these movements have shown in exploiting the new technologies for their political advantage is simply a testimonial to the opportunities opened up by the decentered Panopticon for subversive networking of whatever political stripe.

CLOSING THE BARN DOOR?

The potentially subversive implications of cyberspace have not escaped the attention of closed, authoritarian regimes. Singapore offers a particularly intriguing example of a society that is capitalist with global ambitions and very accommodative to high-tech innovation, yet which has strong authoritarian tendencies with regard to political expression. Singapore is a closely watched society, with high-tech surveillance of the citizenry more in evidence than perhaps anywhere else on earth. For instance, traffic is monitored intensively and regulated by computer control, but pedestrian traffic is also watched electronically and even minor rules infractions, such as littering, are swiftly punished. Singapore wants and needs to have full Internet access to maximise the global business opportunities that real-time networking offers. Yet at the same time Singapore has attempted to control and censor what can be accessed by local users in order to protect the regime from unwelcome and potentially disruptive foreign ideas. Singapore has tried in effect to construct a local Panopticon that is open to global capitalist opportunities but closed to political opportunities. Yet there remain very real questions about the long-term capacity of the Singapore state to actually enforce selective controls over cyberspace: can any one, relatively small state really open up to the wider world in one area while throwing up barriers in another? Cyberspace is perhaps too protean and plastic a medium to be domesticated in this selective a manner. Like the old seaports of the past, cyberspace is a window to the world. Ships might have set sail laden with goods for export, and returned with valuable goods in exchange. But they always brought back the strange and the exotic, the allure of the unknown, and the seeds of subversion with them as well. And of course the seas were vast and foreign ports distant, while in cyberspace things flow back and forth in real-time.

China is another state that has set out to ride the Net, harnessing its potential while trying to curtail its energies. According to a report in the *Financial Times*:

> China yesterday announced a series of regulations to control use of the internet—an attempt to crack down on network users that the Beijing leadership claims are leaking state secrets and disseminating "harmful information." The Chinese government has shown an ambivalent attitude towards the internet in the past, instinctively wary of its potential to

spread subversive information while drawn by its capacity to shoulder technological innovation.[15]

The world's largest country does not as yet have all that many Internet connections. At the time the new regulations were imposed, 620,000 Internet subscriptions had been established. Many of them might be shared by ten or twenty people, covering perhaps one percent of the total population. Nevertheless, dissidents inside and outside China have begun to exploit the potential of the new medium for spreading political discontent. As the *New York Times* commented,

> China's struggle to tame the squirming Internet octopus reflects what many experts see as the government's central conundrum: how to foster economic growth and freedom while keeping tight screws on politics. The security official who announced the new rules, gave no nod to the possible trade-offs. "The safe and effective management of computer information networks," he said, "is a prerequisite for the smooth implementation of the country's modernization drive."[16]

Perhaps the notoriously repressive regime in China can manage where others have failed, but the inherent contradiction in the attraction-repulsion syndrome toward the new technology is striking.

An analogy from the impact of an older technology on another Communist police state is television in the old German Democratic Republic. East Germans could easily receive West German television signals. This posed a serious threat to the fragile legitimacy of an artificial and unpopular state. West German television brought capitalist values directly into East German homes with no linguistic or cultural barriers to reception. The regime could have, of course, prevented the sale of TV sets altogether, but it was unprepared to do this, both because diffusion of TV was a symbol of the GDR's economic "success" and because the regime wanted to utilize the powerful medium as a propaganda tool. The latter was not very successful (an old East German joke went: "What is an 'Ulb'? An Ulb is the unit of power one saves by turning off the TV during a speech by Ulbricht," the then party boss). It was no use tasking the Stasi to compile dossiers on who watched the forbidden stations:

everyone did, and everyone knew everyone did. Punishing trans-gressors at random would have been equally futile. So images of life in the West arrived nightly in the living rooms of the GDR, eroding the isolation that protected the Communist system and luring in-creasing numbers of people to flee westward over the Berlin Wall—until the final collapse of the regime and the reunification of the two Germanies. There were multiple causes for the weakness and ulti-mate collapse of the GDR and its system, among which Western TV would hardly figure near the top. Yet it was like an incessant water drip that slowly but surely erodes a hard surface.

THE INSPECTOR INSPECTED:
THE CYBERNETIC PANOPTICON

Clearly, the precise political implications of the new technologies remain very much in doubt. Optimists point to opportunities opened up by cyberspace and the elastic new frontier of progressive networking. Authoritarian regimes will be challenged, possibly se-verely. Pessimists tend to argue that wealth and power will domi-nate cyberspace, just as they dominate physical space. Pessimists particularly tend to emphasise the ownership structure of the new media and the corporate concentration resulting from the con-vergence of different kinds of enterprises—software companies, computer manufacturers, telephone and cable companies, enter-tainment producers, etc.—in mergers, partnerships, strategic alli-ances, and so on. How, they ask, can we compete with this array of power and influence? Even Orwell puts in a guest appearance, with the U.S. government trying to insist on the cyberspace equivalent of wiretapping privileges.

Perhaps an old joke might be apposite at this point: the optimist happily declares that "we are living in the best of all possible worlds"; the pessimist sadly rejoins that, unfortunately, the opti-mist just may be right. What is clear is that the new information technologies have fundamentally restructured the exercise of pan-optic power. The decentered nature of the "consensual" Panopti-con extends well beyond the diffusion of power at the top along with the participation of the subjects in their own surveillance. It also facilitates unmediated horizontal communication among the pan-optic subjects, and the capacity of the subjects to "watch the watch-ers," to carry out potentially democratic surveillance from below. The enforced isolation and separation of the prisoners in Bentham's Panopticon has been destroyed, the cell walls have crumbled. Not only that, but the Inspector can now himself be inspected. There is tremendous irony here. Bentham imagined an architectural artifice to construct the illusion of an all-knowing, yet unknowable, godlike figure at the center. Today the new technologies offer the substance, as well as the illusion, of omniscience, yet the same technologies relentlessly strip away the shadows that once deliberately obscured the face of power. The one-way transparency of the city of glass is replaced by two-way transparency. The cybernetic model is one of feedback loops bringing about constant adjustments and readjust-ments. The cybernetic Panopticon folds back in on itself.

In *1984*, Winston Smith's job in the Ministry of Truth was to rewrite the historical record constantly, and consign old and no longer politically correct texts to the memory hole. There was a time in the former Soviet Union when the Great Soviet Encyclopedia was constantly being rewritten along Orwellian lines. In one well-known example, an article extolling the infamous secret police chief Lavrenti Beria was ordered removed after the latter's execution and replaced by an article on the "Bering Sea." There are also notorious examples of photographs reworked to remove non-persons — such as a photo of Lenin and Trotsky magically retouched to remove Trotsky altogether. The real totalitarian state was less efficient than its imagined Orwellian construction. Copies of the original photos remained to be compared by critics with the revised ones. Some owners of the Encyclopedia might resist instructions to snip out Beria and add the Bering Sea. In *1984*, all communication and me-dia were so strictly controlled from above that once information was sent down the memory hole, all record of it vanished forever. No real dictatorship has ever held that degree of control. But with the new information technologies, even the degree of control actually exer-cised in the past is rapidly slipping out of anyone's hands. Consider the ease with which information can be picked up from anywhere, downloaded into individual computer files, and simultaneously redirected to any number of other addresses across the globe. Consider that when a communication is being sent to an address in a country that might be sensitive about its citizens receiving such information, the message could be encrypted, in a sufficiently sophisticated code that would render it, if not invulnerable, at least extremely difficult to break. Consider further that if the appearance of an obviously encrypted message might attract unwelcome attention to its recipient, the same information might be sent in the form of a photograph or a piece of music on tape, which with the proper key could be read as a digitally encoded message.[17] Consider finally that these capacities are not the preserve of powerful and secretive state security and intelligence agencies but are open to virtually anyone with a modest amount of funds and a minimal amount of technical proficiency.

We have already pointed to the demonstrated abilities of Third World and indigenous people to seize the opportunities of the new technologies and of global networking as a resistance strategy. As lessons are learned and absorbed, these strategies should become more effective yet. The globalization of capitalism will almost certainly be paralleled by a globalization of resistance networks, as labor unions, feminists, environmentalists, and a host of other groups from civil society network across borders to fight particular issues, only to form and reform in different alliances and partnerships to fight other battles—just as the flexible capitalist enterprise forms and reforms virtual organizations for particular ventures.

Sometimes these popular-resistance groups will form alliances with particular groups of states, or even with particular corporations when there are divisions to be exploited. Take for instance the case of the worldwide campaign against landmines. A cross-border alliance of non-governmental organizations, utilizing such high-profile media personalities as the late Princess Diana, mobilized world opinion and a group of states of middle-power status, led by Canada, that succeeded in establishing a global treaty against landmines, despite the reluctance, if not the opposition, of the United States.

In other cases, resistance will be seen as a threat to capital and will be met by repression, including the surveillance powers of intelligence, security, and police forces. Neither the costs nor the responsibilities for global repressive power will be shouldered by the corporate sector alone. Whatever the precise shape and character of resistance networks, and whatever the responses of global capitalism, it is clear that the configuration of these forces will not amount simply to a new quasifeudalism.

When we look at the international arena, which more closely approaches the anarchic conditions of virtual feudalism, we see something quite different. Transnational corporations are threatened in their global business dealings by "illegitimate" actors whose operations are themselves global in scope: terrorists, some political, some non-political, who attack corporate executives or hold them to ransom, or threaten the security of corporate investments; transnational organized crime that may be in drug traffic, illegal arms trade, gambling, prostitution, or even in legitimate "front" activities; money laundering as an global financing mechanism for all types of illegal activities; and systematic corruption of vulnerable governments. There are eerie parallels between criminal activities and the global economy. Mafias are organized in networks that ignore borders and national jurisdictions, just as transnational corporations tend to operate. They not only utilize the new information technologies to do business, they have restructured their own organizational forms to take advantage of the opportunities of the new technologies: flexibility in seeking out and seizing opportunities, an ability to strike strategic alliances and partnerships, and an ability to dissolve these briskly when they no longer serve a purpose. Finally, they have shown considerable capacity to exploit the new technologies for their own purposes through inventive forms of "cybercrime."

The "global criminal economy," embodied in money laundering, has, in Manuel Castells' words, become a "significant and troubling component of global financial flows and stock markets," but "the impact of crime on state institutions and politics is even greater. State sovereignty, already battered by the processes of globalization . . . is directly threatened by flexible networks of crime that bypass controls, and assume a level of risk that no other organizations are capable of absorbing."[18] But even if directly threatened, states are made even more necessary than ever, precisely because of the threat. In the face of pervasive transborder threats, which we might call the dark side of globalization, "legitimate" private interests are relatively helpless without the assistance of states and their extensive policing, security and intelligence apparatuses, expertise, and enforcement powers.

THE GLOBAL STATE OF NATURE: NASTY, BRUTISH, AND SHORT?

Another historical analogy might be more fruitful. In seventeenth-century Britain, a capitalist mode of agricultural production was replacing the decayed feudal institutions, with peasants being driven off the land. At the same time, mercantile capitalism was also rising in importance, centered in towns linked to wider trading routes. Political structures sometimes lagged behind these economic developments, and political turmoil boiled over into civil wars. Modern English political theory was generated by this context of dislocation and change. Hobbes and Locke were the preeminent figures who, although rather different in their prescriptions, both developed the notion of a social contract underlying and justifying the role of government. Yet while rationalizing and justifying the state, both were "liberal" thinkers concerned about emancipating the new productive forces of the market and, in Locke's case at least, freeing and giving greater expression to the political energies of the new commercial class. Hobbes in particular has been a puzzle for many, because his enthusiastic depiction of government as the "Great Leviathan" and his apparently expansive and sweeping notion of the powers of the sovereign state seem at first glance to rest oddly beside his espousal of market-driven, contractual relations as the basis of a rational society.[19] In fact, Hobbes's seventeenth-century notions of a "Leviathan" state turn out to be pale beside twentieth-century realities: most of what we now consider activity routinely subject to government regulation and intervention, Hobbes assumed would go quite unimpeded by any notice by the state, let alone interference. Still, as the great theorist of sovereignty, Hobbes did much to lay the foundations of the modern notion of the state as the seat of superlative, unchallengeable power and authority. Squaring this theorization of state sovereignty with an emergent free market is not that difficult. For contractual relations to replace the older feudal relations, contracts had to be enforced; as Hobbes lucidly and convincingly argued, the unregulated market alone could not guarantee fulfilment of contractual obligations, or even security of property. Left to its own devices in the "state of nature" without government, the market is a war of all against all, where life is "solitary, poor, nasty, brutish, and short."[20] The way out of this dilemma is the social contract, whereby everyone agrees to transfer their power to the sovereign: a common power over all who can impartially enforce contractual obligations and make the market work. Thus, the historical conjuncture between the rise of capitalism and the relatively strong nation-state.

Today's global economy has freed capitalism from the constraints of the nation-state, and transnational capitalism is making the most of its freedom. But as Hobbes understood, the state not only constrains but protects and enables. Contemporary global economic competition threatens to reproduce some of the conditions of Hobbes' state of nature. Clearly there cannot and will not be any global Leviathan reproducing the terms and conditions of a universalized Hobbesian social contract. As I have tried to indicate, the structural conditions for centralized, absolute sovereign authority have slipped away at the level of the nation-state, let alone on a global scale. Despite the paranoia of some on the American Right, there is no dictatorial World Government under Communist, Zionist, international banker or any other auspices looming on the horizon. To that extent, Mowshowitz is right. But the leap from there back to a recurring feudalism of an epoch prior to Hobbes and prior to the emergence of capitalist market relations is a leap too far. It is rather more likely that the conditions of global competition will require, if not a global Leviathan, as such, then at least a functional equivalent thereof that is appropriately designed for a networked world, perhaps a globalized Panopticon. What might this look like?

BIG BROTHER OUTSOURCED

I argued in an earlier chapter that one of the first redundancies occasioned by the advent of the participatory Panopticon was Big Brother. The new technologies of surveillance made his services to the nation-state obsolete. Real-life Hitlers and Stalins have passed into history, but so has the idealized image of the omniscient, omnipotent totalitarian dictator. Dispersed panoptic power decenters the state. A networked world is a world in which power is networked, diffused into nodes located at key network intersections. At most, we might imagine regional dictators manning some of these nodes, the Saddam Husseins and Slobodan Milosevics of the future.

Technological redundancies sometimes prove self-limiting. Jobs that are removed often reappear as external to the organization, as consultancies, contracts, etc. There is even a word invented to describe this new flexible employment plan that parallels downsizing or "rightsizing": *outsourcing*. Today, in the face of the challenges of the globalizing economy, and especially the threats posed by globalization's own inherent instabilities and by the rise of the parallel shadow world of global crime and corruption, what I have called the dark side of globalization, Big Brother is being brought back as an outside consultant, as it were.

Why should transnational corporations undertake the huge investments in human and material resources required to equip themselves with a capacity that replicates what large states already possess—and at the same time gird themselves for the intimate, perpetual, and immensely difficult cooperation with their competitors that would be necessary to run an effective global security operation? Why not instead urge their respective states to cooperate closely on their behalf in policing the emergent global economy, so that they can get on with their primary business, making money? That is precisely what transnational corporations are doing at the end of twentieth century, and in the process are encouraging a level of strong state activity and strong state cooperation that directly belies the vision of a world of private fiefs exercising sovereignty over limited areas that virtual feudalism offers.

This is not to say that states will continue to look like states have looked in the past. Already states are recreating themselves along less overarching and more flexible lines. States, which of course are not all equal, with many weak and few strong, may become more specialized entities, retaining functions for which they possess a comparative advantage over the private sector, while dropping others altogether or assigning them to the private sector. Nor will states be in any sense stand-alone entities, rather they, too, will constantly be forming and reforming transnational networks and alliances with other states, with corporations and other private-sector actors, and with non-governmental groups and movements.

One area in which states do have a comparative advantage over corporations is in the exercise of coercion. The technologies of surveillance and repression may be developed in the private sector for profit, but they will be deployed and exercised more by states, and by state networks. Here is where Big Brother comes back as an outsourced consultant. Whether confronting the perceived security threat of immigrants and refugees to the prosperous West with transnational police cooperation, shared data bases, and sophisticated technologies of political control,[21] or deploying against terrorists or suspected terrorists surveillance technologies from spy satellites to communications, intercepts cross-border cooperation in coercion is sophisticated and well developed. These are the kind of things states and state agencies do rather well, and that they will concentrate on and specialize in. But they will not do them as ends in themselves, or as means to the pure self-aggrandizement of the state, as in the old totalitarian idea. Rather the exercise of coercion will be a functional specialization within a complex, networked world.

I began this book with a consideration of the "century of Intelligence." It is only fitting that I bring things to a close with the return of Intelligence as the systematic and purposeful acquisition of secret information. The state has been decentered; power is dispersed and diffused; surveillance has become multidirectional. The participatory Panopticon obviates many, although hardly all, of the coercive elements of older panoptic power. Yet these developments have not eliminated the requirement for a global surveillance regime that supports coercive interventions.[22] Such a regime is required because the networked world contains deep elements of instability and contradiction. It is required because non-state actors such as terrorists threaten the stability of the international state system, not to speak of business and investment. It is required because the networked world is paralleled and challenged by its threatening doppelgänger, the dark side of globalization: transnational organized crime and corruption, drug trafficking, illegal arms sales, money laundering, etc.

In the aftermath of the Cold War, there was some ill-founded speculation about the post–Cold War obsolescence of security and intelligence agencies. That this has not happened has been the cause of some cynicism about critics who sneer at bureaucratic agencies struggling to keep alive their empires and their appropriations by inventing new enemies to replace old enemies gone out of service. There is of course some truth in this, as no bureaucratic agencies ever voluntarily give up their prerogatives and tend to be quite creative to justifying their perpetuation. But the new enemies pointed to by intelligence agencies are not invented, they are all too real. And there are very good grounds for arguing that the profession of Intelligence, and the particular technologies and methods used by these agencies, are what is indeed required to track and interpret and draw maps that describe the networks of criminality and terror that shadow the global economy. Borderless threats will require extensive cross-border cooperation in response, but here too intelligence agencies have extensive experience in alliances and network sharing, experience forged in the Cold war era under the pressures of confronting a perceived common threat emanating from the rival bloc. Threats are now more diffuse, but the experience of the earlier era in forging cross-border networks of surveillance, typically on a direct agency-to-agency basis rather than routed through formal government-to-government relations, offer an interesting paradigm of how these matters will have to be organized in the networked world of the future. In the age of cyberspace, new information technologies enable global networks of criminality to proliferate and threaten the integrity not only of the economic institutions of capitalism but also of the political institutions of democratic states and, most insidiously, their civil societies. The ravages of drug abuse in the inner cities of North America and Europe are evidence enough of the human costs exacted by global criminal cartels. The same technologies offer the means to combat these threats. Big Brother is needed once again, but—and this point must be underlined emphatically—only as a functionally specialized consultant, not to run the show itself.

Terrorism has undoubtedly been misused by governments as an excuse for excessive repression and targeting of particular suspect communities, such as immigrant groups from countries from whence international terrorist activity emanates. That does not mean that terrorism is a threat conjured up by states. And when there exists potential for the proliferation of weapons of mass destruction, whether nuclear, chemical, or biological, not only into the hands of so-called rogue states such as Iraq, but into the hands of violent non-state actors with politico-religious agendas incompatible with any idea of international or even domestic order, there is a problem of the most extreme gravity. There is the grisly example of the millenarian *Aum Shinrikyo* cult in Japan that released deadly sarin gas in three trains in the Tokyo subway system, killing twelve people and injuring 5,000. Groups using more conventional methods of destruction have been responsible for acts such as the bombing of the World Trade Center in New York. The potential power that could be exercised by such groups possessing nuclear devices or chemical or biological agents is not something invented by hysterical states. In attempting to preempt these potential threats, existing apparatuses of surveillance and coercion, themselves networked across borders, will be on the cutting edge. The advanced system for communications interception described earlier[23] will be part of this, as will the global surveillance satellite regime. But even more traditional methods of intelligence gathering, such as the penetration of targeted networks by human agents and sources, are also required.

Take the problem of money laundering, which is a key to unlocking many of the activities of the dark side of globalization. Transnational capital and states alike are threatened by this process that utilizes the new technologies and networking forms to finance criminal activities and to corrupt both governmental and corporate figures. Tracing the money laundering networks is the task of Intelligence, laying charges is the task of police. Neither can be done by national units working in isolation against these transborder activities. The technological means to combat this threat does exist. There is no theoretical limit on the surveillance capacity of contemporary technologies to track financial transactions wherever they occur—assuming global compliance with a reporting regime. In fact, an office of the U.S. Treasury, called FinCen, is right now coordinating such a global effort. When such a surveillance system is complete, every transaction—from personal withdrawals at ATMs to major capital flows—could be tracked. Artificial Intelligence software has been and is being developed to scan this staggeringly vast area of data and to recognize anomalous patterns. When suspicious movements of money are identified, it is then up to the government or governments where suspicious activities are found to be taking place to agree to investigate and prosecute. The technology is not the problem—international cooperation on a global scale is.

Such a global surveillance regime of course raises other issues. Civil libertarians will object to the intrusive eyes peering into people's financial affairs. Transnational corporations, even while recognizing the importance of controlling the global criminal economy, may be loath to subject some of their own less-than-scrupulous financial practices to external scrutiny. Eventually, however, it is the Hobbesian problem of order that has to be addressed. And with it the possibility that other, more "legitimate" elements of potential instability in the global order may also fall under more concerted surveillance and control, such as financial markets and capital flows, matters up to now left to multilateral surveillance mechanisms such as the International Monetary Fund. The idea that governments today are powerless to control instant flows of capital is no doubt true if states are seen as stand-alone entities attempting to exercise autonomous, sovereign powers. A globally networked world does not preclude the possibility of global cooperation on an enforceable economic surveillance regime.[24] The technology is certainly there to do just that, and the motive for ensuring stability against the potential for ruinous volatility is there as well. The will and political capacity are of course more problematic. But the problem has been posed and will remain on the agenda for the future.

POWER SWITCHES

Let us imagine a world in which the nation-state, as presently understood, has indeed declined drastically in capacity and significance, and private economic investment and production decisions are made with even less regard than today for (residual) national boundaries. Political sovereignty has been largely, although probably never entirely, detached from territory and political power is dispersed along multiple nodes that form in the key intersections of the multiple networks, mainly but by no means entirely economic, that trace the skeleton of the global political economy. These nodes are not "national" as such, although some may be more predominantly of one nationality than others. Even those with a relatively strong national color draw much of their strength from their networked linkages to other nodes that often cut across national lines. Nations continue to exist in the cultural and sociological sense, and states continue to exist in certain functional aspects, but the once mighty and potent engine of the nation-state has been largely disaggregated.

This picture departs drastically from the quasi-feudal model in that property is not fixed and immobile but plastic and ambulatory. The institutional base is protean, with organizations perpetually forming and reforming in shifting alliances and partnerships with other organizations. It also differs from feudalism in that political power has *not* been appropriated by private economic interests, although it may be shared in public-private alliances in which specific elements of coercive power are devolved or assigned to private agents or carriers.

As Manuel Castells suggests, a networked world is a source of "dramatic reorganization of power relationships":

> Switches connecting the networks (for example, financial flows taking control of media empires that influence political processes) are the privi-

leged instruments of power. Thus the switchers are the power holders. Since networks are multiple, the interoperating codes and switches between networks become the fundamental sources in shaping, guiding and misguiding societies.[25]

The problem of power and its uses and misuses remains throughout the economic and social transformations wrought by new technologies and new ways of organizing production and distribution of goods and services, and of organizing knowledge and information. What also remains, as open-ended in its own way as the processes of a networked world, is the potential for more democratic control of the switches. The new information technologies have not closed this avenue, they have reshaped the terrain on which future struggles for power will be played out.

NOTES TO CHAPTER 7

1. Abbe Mowshowitz, "Virtual feudalism," in Peter J. Denning and Robert M. Metcalfe, eds., *Beyond Calculation: The Next Fifty Years of Computing* (N.Y.: Springer-Verlag, 1997), 213–31.
2. Mowshowitz, 226.
3. This is the same future, without the "feudal" label, spelled out with relish and enthusiasm by James Dale Davidson and William Rees-Mogg: *The Sovereign Individual: The Coming Economic Revolution, How to Survive and Prosper in It* (London: Macmillan, 1997). Mowshowitz seems to maintain an impartial amorality regarding the immiseration of those left out of the information revolution; Davidson and Rees-Mogg as British Thatcherites welcome it as the just come-uppance of the poor who have had the temerity in the past to expect welfare transfers from the rich.
4. Mowshowitz, 227.
5. C.D. Shearing and P.C. Stenning, *Private Security and Private Justice: A Review of Policy Issues* (Montreal: Institute for Research on Public Policy, 1983).
6. "Zapatista Rebel Supporters Wage Virtual War," *Wired News.* 4 February 1998.
7. Manuel Castells, *The Information Age: Economy, Society and Culture,* vol. 2: *The Power of Identity* (Oxford: Blackwell, 1997), 68–83.
8. Castells, 79.
9. "A Rebel Movement's Life on the Web," *Wired News,* 6 March 1998.
10. Tony Clarke and Maude Barlow, *MAI: The Multilateral Agreement on Investment and the Threat to Canadian Sovereignty* (Toronto: Stoddart, 1997).
11. Madelaine Drohan, "How the Net Killed the MAI: Grassroots Groups Used Their Own Globalization to Derail Deal," *The Globe & Mail* [Toronto], 29 April 1998.
12. Ibid.
13. Edward Rothstein, "Finding Utopia on the Internet," *New York Times,* 27 October 1997.
14. Elizabeth G. Olson, "Nations Struggle With How to Control Hate on the Web," *New York Times,* 24 November 1997.

15. James Harding, "China: Crackdown on Internet 'Subversion,'" *Financial Times*, 31 December 1997.

16. Erik Eckholm, "China Cracks Down on Dissent in Cyberspace," *New York Times*, 31 December 1997.

17. This encryption technique, called Stego, has been developed by one of the more exotic characters in cyberspace, Romana Machado, also known as Cypherella, a former California model who displays her encryption expertise on one website, and her more personal charms on another, erotic, website.

18. Manuel Castells, *The Information Age*, v. 3: *End of Millennium* (Oxford: Blackwell, 1998), 201–2.

19. C. B. Macpherson, *The Political Theory of Possessive Individualism*: Hobbs to Locke (Oxford: Clarenden Press, 1962).

20. Hobbes, *Leviathan* Part II, Chapter 13. (Hammondsworth, Middlesex: Penguin Books, 1968).

21. This is certainly the case in "Fortress Europe": Michael Spencer, *States of Injustice: A Guide to Human Rights and Civil Liberties in the European Union* (London: Pluto Press, 1995); Tony Bunyan, ed., *Statewatching the New Europe* (Nottingham: Russell Press, 1993); Steve Wright, *An Appraisal of Technologies for Political Control* (Luxembourg: European Parliament, Directorate General for Research, 1998).

22. Stephen Gill, "The Global Panopticon? The Neoliberal State, Economic Life, and Democratic Surveillance," *Alternatives* 2 (1995): 1–49.

23. See Chapter Four.

24. The Asian financial meltdown in 1997/98 has led even some noted neoliberal economists to wonder aloud whether the IMF"s traditional role in forcing governments to adopt neoliberal policies might not better be replaced by a body prepared to regulate financial markets and institutions, rather than bailing out institutions after they have failed.

25. Castells, *Information Age*, v. 1: *The Rise of the Network Society* (Oxford: Blackwell, 1996), 471.

—Index